The Marvelous Wonderettes

Written & Created by
Roger Bean

The Marvelous Wonderettes
is dedicated to Lois Bean

STEELE SPRING
STAGE RIGHTS
www.stagerights.com

THE MARVELOUS WONDERETTES

For all stage performance inquiries, please contact:

Steele Spring Stage Rights
3845 Cazador Street
Los Angeles, CA 90065
(323) 739-0413
www.stagerights.com

ORIGINAL PRODUCTION NOTES

Written and Created by Roger Bean

The Marvelous Wonderettes opened off-Broadway on September 14, 2008,
at the Westside Theatre, presented by
David Elzer, Peter Schneider, Roger Bean and Marvelous NYC LLC.

Musical Arrangements and Direction by Brian William Baker
Orchestrations by Michael Borth
Vocal Arrangements by Brian William Baker & Roger Bean
Scenic Design by Michael Carnahan
Costume Design by Bobby Pearce
Lighting Design by Jeremy Pivnick
Sound Design by Cricket Myers
Stage Managed by Andrew Neal
Choreography by Janet Miller
Directed by Roger Bean

Cast
Farah Alvin ....Missy
Beth Malone ....Betty Jean
Bets Malone........................ Suzy
Victoria Matlock..........Cindy Lou

Original Off-Broadway Cast Album Available on PS Classics
Vocal Selections Available from Alfred Music

The Los Angeles production premiered on September 29, 2006,
at the El Portal Forum Theatre, North Hollywood, CA, presented by
David Elzer, Peter Schneider, Roger Bean, and Marvelous Dreams LLC
with Kirsten Chandler, Kim Huber, Julie Dixon Jackson, and Bets Malone.

Originally produced in 1999 and 2001 by Milwaukee Repertory Theater
Joseph Hanreddy, Artistic Director, Timothy J. Shields, Managing Director
with Laurie Birmingham, Bets Malone, Jacquelyn Ritz,
Becky Spice, and Rae Ann Theriault.

CAST OF CHARACTERS

CINDY LOU (18, 28) knows she is the prettiest girl at Springfield High. She assumes she will be named Prom Queen and acts out against best friend Betty Jean when things don't go her way. She makes the biggest change between Acts I and II, having learned the lessons of true love and loss. Cindy Lou wears pink.

MISSY (18, 28) is the over-achiever of the group. Very controlled and controlling, and extremely concerned that everything at the prom turns out wonderful and perfect. An elementary school teacher in-the-making, she is head of the prom decorations committee, and absolutely smitten with her music teacher, Mr. Lee. Her best friend is Suzy. Missy wears orange/apricot.

BETTY JEAN (18, 28) is the class clown and tomboy, always vying for attention with her best friend Cindy Lou. It's highly probably that Betty Jean wants to be with Cindy Lou herself, but doesn't even know what those feelings really are. Cindy Lou steals Betty Jean's boyfriend away, which causes a lot of the friction at the prom. She holds a grudge against Cindy Lou until they make up at the 10-year reunion. Betty Jean wears green.

SUZY (18, 28) is sometimes stereotyped as the ditzy blonde because she is always smiling and giggling— nothing ever seems to bother her. Suzy is in love with the lighting operator, Ritchie Stevens, and completely surprised when named prom queen. Her bets friend is Missy. Frustrated, sad, hormonal, and pregnant in Act II. Suzy wears blue.

MUSICAL NUMBERS

ACT I – THE PROM (1958)

1. Mr. Sandman...Ensemble
2. Sugar and Spice Medley:
   Lollipop ....Ensemble
   Sugartime...Ensemble
3. Chipmunk Cheer ....Ensemble
4. Allegheny Moon...Ensemble
5. Dream Medley:
   All I Have to Do is Dream ....Ensemble
   Dream Lover...Ensemble
6. Stupid Cupid ....Suzy
7. Lipstick on Your Collar ....Betty Jean
8. Lucky Lips ....Cindy Lou
9. Secret Love...Missy
10. Man of My Dreams Medley:
    Mr. Lee .... Missy, Ensemble
    Born Too Late..Ensemble
    Teacher's Pet ....Ensemble
11. Sugar and Spice Reprise ....[Prom Queen Voting]
12. Goodnight and Goodbye Medley:
    Sincerely...Ensemble
    Goodnight Sweetheart..Ensemble
13. Hold Me, Thrill Me, Kiss Me .... Suzy, Ensemble

MUSICAL NUMBERS (CONT'D)

<u>ACT II – THE REUNION (1968)</u>

14. Heatwave .... Ensemble
15. Mr. Sandman Reprise .... Ensemble
16. It's in His Kiss/Wedding Bell Blues .... Missy, Ensemble
17. You Don't Own Me .... Missy, Ensemble
18. With This Ring.. Missy, Ensemble
19. I Only Want to Be With You ....Betty Jean, Ensemble
20. That's When the Tears Start..Betty Jean, Ensemble
21. It's My Party ....Betty Jean, Ensemble
22. Son of a Preacher Man ....Cindy Lou, Ensemble
23. Leader of the Pack ....Cindy Lou, Ensemble
24. Maybe ....Cindy Lou, Ensemble
25. Suzy's Medley:
       Maybe .... Suzy, Ensemble
       Needle in a Haystack.................................. Missy, Cindy Lou, Betty Jean
       Rescue Me .... Suzy, Ensemble
       Respect .... Suzy, Ensemble
26. Thank You and Goodnight .... Ensemble
27. Bows .... Ensemble
28. Exit Music .... Ensemble

TIME AND PLACE

Springfield High School Gymnasium, USA
Act I: Class of 1958's Super Senior Prom
Act II: 1968, the Class of 1958's Ten-Year Reunion

RUN TIME

Act I is approximately 50 minutes.
Act II is approximately 48 minutes.

ADDITONAL VERSIONS

The following versions of *The Marvelous Wonderettes*
are also available from Stage Rights:

The Marvelous Wonderettes (Glee Club Edition)

In this version, our four Wonderettes are joined onstage by
the Springfield High Chipmunk Glee Club— as many girls
(and boys!) as needed. 55 minutes in length.

The Marvelous Wonderettes '58

Make it home by curfew in this delightful one-act (the
senior prom) version of the smash off-Broadway hit.
55 minutes in length.

ACT I

1958, SPRINGFIELD, USA.

We are in a high school gymnasium, and the stage is set for the 1958 Senior Prom, complete with banners, streamers, and signs. There is a large platform up center with steps on each side; this is the "stage" that has been set up for tonight's performance. Behind, there are cascades of pastel streamers descending from a portal of hearts with banners that read: "Class Of 1958 Super Senior Prom," and the theme of the prom: "Marvelous Dreams." There are swinging doors leading into the boys' and girls' locker rooms on either side, as well as two decorated tables of refreshments. There are four microphones on stands with heart boxes on them.

Somewhere on the wall of the gymnasium should be a classic framed portrait of the President of the United States (Eisenhower), perhaps with a flag nearby. This will help set the time period for the audience.

Throughout the show, the girls sing back-up vocals for each song, which may not be indicated in lyrics.

As the lights fade to black, we hear a mini-overture, before being cut off by the school buzzer. The four girls enter as we hear:

PRINCIPAL (V.O.): Students of Springfield High School, this is Principal Varney. Welcome to your 1958 Super Senior Prom!

MISSY *(whispering)*: Careful!

SUZY *(kicking step)*: Whoops!

PRINCIPAL (V.O.): What a great evening we're having. And to top it all off, we have some terrific entertainment for you. So hang onto your corsages, and welcome to the stage your very own Marvelous Wonderettes!

SONG #1: MR. SANDMAN

The lights come up on CINDY LOU, BETTY JEAN, MISSY and SUZY at the microphones, dressed in formal prom gowns. MISSY wears cat-eye glasses; SUZY chews gum throughout.

It is suggested to keep the girls color-coordinated in both acts: CINDY LOU wears pink, BETTY JEAN wears green, MISSY wears orange (apricot), and SUZY wears blue. These colors match their characters and personalities.

ALL:

BUM, BUM, BUM, BUM, BUM, BUM, BUM, BUM

BUM, BUM, BUM, BUM, BUM

SUZY giggles.

BUM, BUM, BUM, BUM, BUM, BUM, BUM, BUM

BUM, BUM, BUM, BUM, BUM

MR. SANDMAN, BRING ME A DREAM

MAKE HIM THE CUTEST THAT I'VE EVER SEEN

GIVE HIM TWO LIPS LIKE ROSES IN CLOVER

THEN TELL HIM THAT HIS LONESOME NIGHTS ARE OVER

SANDMAN, I'M SO ALONE

DON'T HAVE NOBODY TO CALL MY OWN

PLEASE TURN ON YOUR MAGIC BEAM

MR. SANDMAN, BRING ME A DREAM

BUM, BUM, BUM, BUM, BUM, BUM, BUM, BUM

BUM, BUM, BUM, BUM, BUM (BUM)

BUM, BUM, BUM, BUM, BUM, BUM, BUM, BUM

BUM, BUM, BUM, BUM, BUM

CINDY LOU:

MR. SANDMAN, BRING ME A DREAM

MAKE HIM THE CUTEST THAT I'VE EVER SEEN

GIVE HIM THE WORD THAT I'M NOT A ROVER

THEN TELL HIM THAT HIS LONESOME NIGHTS ARE OVER

SANDMAN, I'M SO ALONE

DON'T HAVE NOBODY TO CALL MY OWN

PLEASE TURN ON YOUR MAGIC

ALL:

BEAM, WAH

MR. SANDMAN, BRING ME A DREAM

BUM, BUM, BUM, BUM, BUM, BUM, BUM, BUM

BUM, BUM, BUM, BUM, BUM (BUM)

BUM, BUM, BUM, BUM, BUM, BUM, BUM, BUM

BUM, BUM, BUM, BUM, BUM

MR. SANDMAN

RITCHIE'S VOICE (V.O.): Yes?

SUZY waves to Ritchie out front, excited.

SUZY: That's Richie! Hi honey!

Ritchie responds to SUZY with a flash of the lights. BETTY JEAN laughs and gets confused, CINDY LOU sings on and MISSY admonishes SUZY.

MISSY: Suzy— pay attention!

CINDY LOU:
GIVE HIM A PAIR OF

CINDY LOU & MISSY:
EYES WITH A

CINDY LOU, MISSY & BETTY JEAN:
COME-HITHER GLEAM

ALL:
GIVE HIM A LONELY HEART LIKE PALLIACHI
AND LOTS OF WAVY HAIR LIKE LIBERACE

MISSY *(quietly, to the others)*: Breathe!

They all take a small, loud breath, letting it out during the following.

ALL:
MR. SANDMAN, SOMEONE TO HOLD
WOULD BE SO PEACHY BEFORE WE'RE TOO OLD
PLEASE TURN ON YOUR MAGIC BEAM
MR. SANDMAN, BRING US
PLEASE, PLEASE, PLEASE
MR. SANDMAN, BRING US A DREAM

Applause.

SUZY curtseys and says "Thank you," as she does after each song in Act I, each with a different attitude based on each situation.

CINDY LOU: Hi everyone! Welcome to our super senior prom! I'm Cindy Lou.

BETTY JEAN: I'm B. J.

MISSY hits her, admonishing.

Ow. Sorry. I'm Betty Jean.

MISSY: I'm Missy.

SUZY: I'm Suzy.

CINDY LOU: And we're...

ALL: The Wonderettes! *(They strike their Wonderettes pose with a noise)* Hhmmm!

MISSY *(whispering)*: Marvelous. Marvelous...

Each of the girls reacts.

CINDY LOU: Oh that's right! We're...

ALL: The Marvelous Wonderettes. *(They point to the banner, then strike their pose again, each move accompanied by the noise)* Hhmmm, hhmmm!

SUZY: They got it. I think they got it.

BETTY JEAN *(to Missy)*: What's next?

MISSY *(whispering to the girls)*: Lollipop... Lollipop...!

> *SUZY gets out her pitch pipe. MISSY sets her bag, then points to SUZY. SUZY blows the first note for <u>LOLLIPOP</u>. MISSY pushes BETTY JEAN out of the way, then SUZY pushes BETTY JEAN out of the way. They face back to begin the song. Now in her place at the end, BETTY JEAN needs to hear the note again from SUZY.*
>
> *SUZY plays a double-note, takes out her gum, then plays one note. MISSY taps on CINDY LOU's shoulder to turn around and begin.*

SONG #2: SUGAR AND SPICE MEDLEY:

[LOLLIPOP]

> *CINDY LOU begins clapping and the girls add on. The song begins a capella. They turn forward as they sing.*

CINDY LOU:
LOLLIPOP, LOLLIPOP, OH-LOLLI LOLLI LOLLI

MISSY *(describing the dance step)*: Cross, turn.

CINDY LOU & MISSY:
LOLLIPOP, LOLLIPOP, OH-LOLLI LOLLI LOLLI

CINDY LOU, MISSY & SUZY:
LOLLIPOP, LOLLIPOP, OH-LOLLI LOLLI LOLLI

ALL:
LOLLIPOP

BETTY JEAN:
POP!

> *Music in. MISSY gets out large wooden lollipops to dance with, and passes them down the line.*

ALL:
LOLLIPOP, LOLLIPOP, OH-LOLLI LOLLI LOLLI
LOLLIPOP, LOLLIPOP, OH-LOLLI LOLLI LOLLI
LOLLIPOP, LOLLIPOP, OH-LOLLI LOLLI LOLLI
LOLLIPOP

BETTY JEAN:
(SLURP)

ALL:
CALL MY BABY LOLLIPOP, TELL YOU WHY
CINDY LOU:
HIS KISS IS SWEETER THAN APPLE PIE
ALL:
AND WHEN HE DOES HIS SHAKIN' ROCKIN' DANCE
MAN I HAVEN'T GOT A CHANCE
CINDY LOU:
I CALL HIM
LOLLIPOP, LOLLIPOP, OH-LOLLI LOLLI LOLLI
MISSY: And...
CINDY LOU & MISSY:
LOLLIPOP, LOLLIPOP, OH-LOLLI LOLLI LOLLI
CINDY LOU, MISSY & SUZY:
LOLLIPOP, LOLLIPOP, OH-LOLLI LOLLI LOLLI
ALL:
LOLLIPOP
BETTY JEAN:
(RAZZBERRY)

SUZY giggles.

ALL:
SWEETER THAN CANDY ON A STICK
HUCKLEBERRY, CHERRY OR LIME
IF YOU HAD A CHOICE HE'D BE YOUR PICK
CINDY LOU:
BUT LOLLIPOP IS MINE

They clip their lollipops to the microphone stands, now singing into the lollipops until the end of SUGARTIME.

ALL:
LOLLIPOP, LOLLIPOP, OH-LOLLI LOLLI LOLLI
LOLLIPOP, LOLLIPOP, OH-LOLLI LOLLI LOLLI
LOLLIPOP, LOLLIPOP, OH-LOLLI LOLLI LOLLI
LOLLIPOP

BETTY JEAN begins to make an "underarm fart" with her hand cupped under her armpit and the others stop her.

*Spoken quickly in succession, topping each other:

*CINDY LOU: Hey!

*MISSY: Stop!

*SUZY: Don't!

BETTY JEAN: What?!

[SUGARTIME]

ALL:
WELL
SUGAR IN THE MORNING, SUGAR IN THE EVENING
SUGAR AFTER SUPPERTIME
BE MY LITTLE SUGAR AND LOVE ME ALL THE TIME

HONEY IN THE MORNING, HONEY IN THE EVENING
HONEY AFTER SUPPERTIME
BE MY LITTLE HONEY AND LOVE ME ALL THE TIME

SUZY:
PUT YOUR ARMS AROUND ME
AND SWEAR BY THE STARS ABOVE
YOU'LL BE MINE FOREVER IN A HEAVEN OF LOVE

ALL:
SUGAR IN THE MORNING, SUGAR IN THE EVENING
SUGAR AFTER SUPPERTIME
BE MY LITTLE SUGAR AND LOVE ME ALL THE TIME

MISSY:
NOW SUGARTIME

BETTY JEAN, CINDY LOU & SUZY:
SUGARTIME

MISSY:
IS ANY TIME

CINDY LOU:
THAT YOU'RE NEAR

BETTY JEAN, MISSY & SUZY:
THAT YOU'RE NEAR

CINDY LOU:
'CAUSE YOU'RE SO DEAR

BETTY JEAN:
SO DON'T YOU ROAM

CINDY LOU, MISSY & SUZY:
DON'T ROAM

BETTY JEAN:
JUST BE MY HONEYCOMB

CINDY LOU:
HONEYCOMB

MISSY:
HONEYCOMB

SUZY:
WE'LL LIVE IN A HEAVEN OF LOVE

MISSY: Right, left.

ALL:

> SUGAR IN THE MORNING, SUGAR IN THE EVENING
> SUGAR AFTER SUPPERTIME
> BE MY LITTLE SUGAR AND LOVE ME ALL THE TIME
> WELL

> *They take an audible gasp of air.*

> WELL
> SUGAR IN THE MORNING, SUGAR IN THE EVENING
> SUGAR AFTER SUPPERTIME
> BE MY LITTLE SUGAR AND LOVE ME ALL THE TIME
> I CALL HIM LOLLIPOP, LOLLIPOP (POP) LOLLIPOP!

> *They turn their lollipops around to reveal the letters L-O-V-E. However, they're in the reverse order, spelling E-V-O-L.*

> *MISSY ad-libs as she quickly rearranges the girls.*

MISSY: Oh! Wrong order, girls!

> *When all in place, with lollipops turned backwards...*

> Pop it, pop it...!

> *They then reveal the proper order of the lollipops, with popping noises again.*

SUZY: It spells love.

> *MISSY gathers the lollipops.*

> They got it. I think they got it.

CINDY LOU: A special thank you to my boss, Mr. Johnson, down at the Springfield Sweet Shoppe for allowing us to use these marvelous lollipops from his window display.

BETTY JEAN: Thank you, Mr. Johnson!

MISSY: Yes— you're the sweetest!

CINDY LOU: So as I said before, we're The Wonderettes.

MISSY *(whispering)***:** Marvelous. Marvelous...

> *BETTY JEAN also jumps in to correct CINDY LOU.*

BETTY JEAN: Marvelous!

CINDY LOU: Oh, that's right. The Marvelous Wonderettes.

> *They all quickly point to the banner then strike their pose, accompanied by two distinct noises.*

ALL: Hhmmm, hhmmm.

CINDY LOU: But— you know us better as the trophy-winning Springfield High School Song Leaders!

BETTY JEAN: Go Chipmunks!!

MISSY: And for those of you who haven't heard by now...

CINDY LOU: And with B.J. around, who hasn't heard?

BETTY JEAN: Go Chipmunks!!

MISSY: We took 3rd place at state again!

> *SUZY holds up a trophy.*

SUZY: Look everyone! Look!

> *They all "ooh" at the trophy. BETTY JEAN has brought a stool center, and SUZY puts the trophy on it.*

BETTY JEAN: Take that, Chess Club! *(She points at someone, makes a chess move, knocking over the King)* Check and mate.

MISSY: A big, huge, amazing, very special thank you to our very special song leader leader, Mr. Lee!

> *She indicates a man in the front row. This audience member is now Mr. Lee throughout the play.*

ALL: Thank you Mr. Lee!

> *They all raise their hands to their faces (like paws) and make chipmunk faces at him, making chipmunk noises as they gnash their teeth.*

BETTY JEAN: Let's show 'em how we won 3rd place!

CINDY LOU: Do you think?

BETTY JEAN: Go Chipmunks!

> *They move into a line. SUZY pulls out the pitch pipe and plays a double-non-note.*

SUZY: Ready?!

ALL: Okay!

SONG #3: CHIPMUNK CHEER

> *(Singing)*
> CHIPMUNK, CHIPMUNK, FLIP YOUR LITTLE TAIL
> CHIPMUNK PRIDE WILL NEVER, EVER FAIL
> WE'RE THE TEAM YOU WON'T DEFEAT
> WE'RE THE RODENTS YOU CAN'T BEAT
> CHIPMUNK, CHIPMUNK, FLIP YOUR LITTLE TAIL

> *They make the sound of a vocal drum roll.*

MISSY:
> WE'LL CLIMB YOUR TREE

SUZY:
  WE'LL PICK YOUR NUTS
CINDY LOU:
  WE'RE HERE TO SAY
BETTY JEAN:
  WE'LL KICK YOUR BUTTS!
ALL:
  GOOOOOOO———— CHIPMUNKS!

> *They show Mr. Lee their chipmunk faces.*
>
> *Applause.*
>
> *BETTY JEAN grabs the trophy.*

BETTY JEAN: Hey— I'm gonna go put it in the trophy case right now!

MISSY: Betty Jean...

BETTY JEAN: Don't do anything without me!

> *BETTY JEAN runs out into the lobby, taking the trophy with her.*
>
> *CINDY LOU, SUZY, and MISSY move mics into place.*
>
> *CINDY LOU sees an opening, and moves her mic into position.*

CINDY LOU (*quickly, before Betty Jean comes back*): Now it's time to sing a song that we learned in Mr. Lee's 4th period choir class.

MISSY: Cindy Lou...!

SUZY: You can't do that.

MISSY: That's Betty Jean's song!

SUZY: You'll get in trouble...!

CINDY LOU: No I won't and yes I can. You just sing your part. Music!

> *As she turns out, the music begins.*

SONG #4: ALLEGHENY MOON

  (*Singing*)
  ALLEGHENY MOON, WE NEED YOUR LIGHT
  TO HELP US FIND ROMANCE TONIGHT

> *BETTY JEAN returns. She is surprised and upset that this song has started without her. She ad-libs her way back onto the stage.*

BETTY JEAN: Ha, ha. Very funny. Start over.

CINDY LOU, MISSY & SUZY:
  SO SHINE, SHINE, SHINE ON TONIGHT

BETTY JEAN: Hey! This is supposed to be my song...!

> *CINDY LOU ignores her. BETTY JEAN tries to get support from MISSY and SUZY, then exits.*

CINDY LOU:
ALLEGHENY MOON, YOUR SILVER BEAMS
CAN LEAD THE WAY TO GOLDEN DREAMS
CINDY LOU, MISSY & SUZY:
SO SHINE, SHINE, PLEASE SHINE
CINDY LOU:
HIGH AMONG THE STARS SO BRIGHT ABOVE
THE MAGIC OF YOUR LAMP OF LOVE

> *BETTY JEAN returns, bringing a "moon on a stick" and placing it behind CINDY LOU. BETTY JEAN joins MISSY and SUZY in the vocal backup.*

CINDY LOU, MISSY & SUZY:
CAN MAKE HIM MINE
CINDY LOU:
ALLEGHENY MOON, IT'S UP TO YOU
PLEASE SEE WHAT YOU CAN DO
FOR ME AND MY ONE AND ONLY LOVE
ALLEGHENY MOON...

> *BETTY JEAN pulls out a harmonica and plays a solo, upsetting CINDY LOU.*

ALL:
SO SHINE, SHINE, SHINE ON TONIGHT
CINDY LOU:
ALLEGHENY MOON...

> *BETTY JEAN plays again.*
>
> *CINDY LOU and BETTY JEAN square off before CINDY LOU recovers and sings again for her audience.*

ALL:
AH, AH, AHHH

> *BETTY JEAN pulls MISSY and SUZY over to sing directly behind CINDY LOU.*

CINDY LOU:
HIGH AMONG THE STARS SO BRIGHT ABOVE
THE MAGIC OF YOUR LAMP OF LOVE
ALL:
CAN MAKE HIM MINE

> *BETTY JEAN "releases" the moon, which slowly descends from the top of the stick over and in front of CINDY LOU.*

CINDY LOU:
> ALLEGHENY MOON, IT'S UP TO YOU
> PLEASE SEE WHAT YOU CAN DO
> FOR ME AND FOR MY ONE AND ONLY LOVE

>> *CINDY LOU grabs the moon and poses with it. She leads the final set of vocals a capella.*

ALL:
> SHINE ON ME TONIGHT—
> ALLEGHENY

>> *CINDY LOU lets go of the moon as it rises up to sit perfectly over her head for the final pose.*

> MOON

>> *Applause.*

>> *MISSY sets microphones for the next song.*

>> *CINDY LOU grabs the moon, glaring at BETTY JEAN. BETTY JEAN places her hands on it as well, and they start to shake the "moon on a stick."*

>> *SUZY rushes over and grabs it from them.*

SUZY: Hey! They can see you!

>> *SUZY takes the moon away. CINDY LOU and BETTY JEAN look out at the audience, smile, and then rush over to the refreshment table, giggling and chattering. BETTY JEAN blows a noisy raspberry on CINDY LOU's arm.*

>> *MISSY gets everyone's attention.*

MISSY: Attention. Eyes. *(After a quick check that everyone is paying attention, she moves forward)* Tonight's entertainment was supposed to be provided by the boys from the glee club...

SUZY: You know: the "Crooning Crab Cakes."

MISSY: Yes, the "Crooning Crab Cakes." But Billy Ray Patton, the lead crab, got suspended from school again.

SUZY: They caught him hanging out behind the girls' locker room. Smoking!!

MISSY & SUZY: Euw!

SUZY: And last Sunday, his dad, the minister, caught him smoking behind the chapel.

MISSY & SUZY: Double-Euw! *(They chant together with gestures)* Tobacco can kill, and make you ill.

SUZY: So don't be a butthead.

BETTY JEAN: Ha! Butthead! She said butthead at the prom!

MISSY: Betty Jean...!

> *MISSY prompts SUZY to continue while she crosses to chastise BETTY JEAN.*

Suzy...

SUZY: Oh. Okay. So Billy Ray Patton is the leader of the "Crooning Crab Cakes," you know, the boys from the glee club, and the "Crooning Crab Cakes" were supposed to sing tonight, but Billy Ray got kicked out of school for being a butthead...

MISSY: Suzy!

BETTY JEAN: Butthead...!

MISSY: Betty Jean!

SUZY: ...so Mrs. Carter, Judy's mom, convinced Mr. Lee and the P.T.A. board that it would be a really bad influence on all of the good kids if the "Crooning Crab Cakes" still got to sing at the prom, since the lead crab got in trouble for being a butthead...

MISSY: Suzy!

BETTY JEAN: Butthead...!

MISSY: Betty Jean!

SUZY: ...so the Crab Cakes got cancelled, Mr. Lee called Missy's mom, who called my mom, who called everybody else's mom, and here we are. *(Posing with her hands up)* Ta da!

BETTY JEAN, CINDY LOU & MISSY *(mimicking the pose)*: Ta da.

SUZY: I mean, my golly, if the boys can do it, so can we.

> *She stands, smiling out, giggling.*

MISSY *(to Suzy)*: Psst. Psst.

> *MISSY holds up her skirt, indicating her dress.*

SUZY: Oh. Okay. So when Mr. Lee asked us to sing for the prom... *(Excited, back to the others)* ...for the prom!

BETTY JEAN, CINDY LOU & MISSY *(also excited)*: The prom!

> *They all squeal together.*

SUZY: ...well, we knew we had to do something extra special. So Missy made our dresses. Aren't they neat-o?

MISSY *(with a curtsey)*: 3rd Period Home Ec. Thank you so much.

> *MISSY runs off and brings on a rolling chalkboard. On the chalkboard is written in stacked words: "Springfield High School Is Just Terrific."*

SUZY: And of course you already heard Ritchie, who's running the lights. Hi Ritchie!

> *She waves to him.*

The lights flash in response.

MISSY: Suzy!

The lights restore.

MISSY begins to erase the writing on the chalkboard. She erases from right to left.

CINDY LOU: Now the theme of tonight's super senior prom is "Marvelous Dreams."

BETTY JEAN: Chosen by Miss McPherson's 3rd period French class!

They all point to Miss McPherson down front. This audience member now becomes Miss McPherson throughout the show.

MISSY turns from erasing the board.

MISSY: Merci, Miss McPherson.

They all quickly give Miss McPherson their own version of a French thank you.

BETTY JEAN: Beaucoup, beaucoup.

CINDY LOU: Oui, oui, oui.

SUZY: Croissant.

MISSY turns back to the chalkboard to see that the only letters she left un-erased spell out S-H-I-T vertically.

MISSY yelps and quickly erases the bad word. SUZY and BETTY JEAN crack up.

CINDY LOU gets their attention by mimicking MISSY.

CINDY LOU: Attention— Eyes!

SUZY and BETTY JEAN stop and listen.

Our marvelous dreams are about the four-letter word that's okay to say.

MISSY has drawn a large heart on the chalkboard before joining the others down front.

It's something we're all searching for— some of us have had better luck than others, do you think?

She glances quickly to BETTY JEAN.

You know what I'm talking about— all of our marvelous dreams are about... love.

On the word love, they each pull out the paper-string hearts from the microphone stands, and connect them together.

SONG #5: DREAM MEDLEY:

[ALL I HAVE TO DO IS DREAM]

ALL:
DREAM, DREAM, DREAM, DREAM
DREAM, DREAM, DREAM, DREAM

WHEN I WANT YOU IN MY ARMS
WHEN I WANT YOU, AND ALL YOUR CHARMS
WHENEVER I WANT YOU, ALL I HAVE TO DO IS
DREAM, DREAM, DREAM, DREAM

WHEN I FEEL BLUE IN THE NIGHT
AND I NEED YOU TO HOLD ME TIGHT
WHENEVER I WANT YOU, ALL I HAVE TO DO IS
DREAM

I CAN MAKE YOU MINE
TASTE YOUR LIPS OF WINE
ANYTIME, NIGHT OR DAY
ONLY TROUBLE IS, GEE WHIZ
I'M DREAMING MY LIFE AWAY

I NEED YOU SO, THAT I COULD DIE
I LOVE YOU SO, AND THAT IS WHY
WHENEVER I WANT YOU, ALL I HAVE TO DO IS
DREAM, DREAM, DREAM, DREAM, DREAM

Each girl moves into the spotlight for her solo.

[DREAM LOVER]

MISSY:
EVERY NIGHT I HOPE AND PRAY
A DREAM LOVER WILL COME MY WAY
A BOY TO HOLD IN MY ARMS
AND KNOW THE MAGIC OF HIS CHARMS
ALL:
BECAUSE I WANT A BOY TO CALL MY OWN
I WANT A DREAM LOVER
SO I DON'T HAVE TO BE ALONE

SUZY:
> DREAM LOVER, WHERE ARE YOU
> WITH THE LOVE THAT'S OH SO TRUE?
> AND THE HAND, THAT I CAN HOLD
> TO FEEL YOU NEAR, WHEN I GROW OLD

ALL:
> BECAUSE I WANT A BOY TO CALL MY OWN
> I WANT A DREAM LOVER,
> SO I DON'T HAVE TO BE ALONE

BETTY JEAN:
> SOMEDAY, I DON'T KNOW HOW
> I HOPE YOU HEAR MY PLEA
> SOMEWAY, I DON'T KNOW HOW

ALL:
> HE'LL BRING HIS LOVE TO ME

> > *CINDY LOU moves up to BETTY JEAN to try to get her out of the way for her solo.*

CINDY LOU: Move!

> *(Singing)*

> DREAM LOVER, UNTIL THEN
> I'LL GO TO SLEEP AND DREAM AGAIN

> > *BETTY JEAN has gotten a bottle of bubbles from the refreshment table, and blows bubbles over CINDY LOU's head from behind.*

> THAT'S THE ONLY THING TO DO
> UNTIL I KNOW IT, DREAMS COME TRUE

ALL:
> BECAUSE I WANT A BOY TO CALL MY OWN
> I WANT A DREAM LOVER
> SO I DON'T HAVE TO BE ALONE

> > *MISSY and SUZY continue singing back-up as CINDY LOU argues with BETTY JEAN about the bubbles.*

CINDY LOU: Give me those bubbles.

BETTY JEAN: What bubbles?

CINDY LOU: We were saving those for later.

BETTY JEAN: Well I wanna use 'em now!

> > *CINDY LOU grabs at the bubbles, and BETTY JEAN holds them away, and then runs up and over the platform, with CINDY LOU close behind. They run back around MISSY and SUZY, breaking through the strings of paper hearts as they run back toward their microphones.*

Throughout, their argument escalates in intensity and volume, with MISSY and SUZY also moving from their spots and joining in. The noise turns into a cacophony.

MISSY ends it with:

MISSY: Sing!

ALL:

BECAUSE I WANT A BOY TO CALL MY OWN

I WANT A DREAM LOVER

SO I DON'T HAVE TO BE ALONE

There is another quick, loud argument, with CINDY LOU pushing BETTY JEAN out of the spotlight. They all speak together:

CINDY LOU: Give me those bubbles now, Betty Jean!

BETTY JEAN: Leave me alone! You can't have them!

MISSY: Stop it! You're both ruining the song!

SUZY: I can't believe you can't be nice for one whole night.

ALL:

DREAM LOVER

I DON'T WANT TO BE ALONE

They take four final poses, BETTY JEAN blowing one final bubble over CINDY LOU's head for the button.

Applause.

MISSY confronts BETTY JEAN, taking away the bubble container.

MISSY: Are you going to ruin the entire evening?

BETTY JEAN: You always blame me! She started it...

MISSY: Betty Jean. Be marvelous.

BETTY JEAN starts to protest, but then takes her "marvelous" pose. MISSY crosses to the front microphone.

BETTY JEAN reaches over and makes MISSY's dress "fart" as she walks away. CINDY LOU and SUZY giggle.

(To the audience)

Attention. Eyes.

MISSY turns front. BETTY JEAN makes a "fart" noise one last time into her microphone. CINDY LOU and SUZY giggle. MISSY continues.

Later on this evening, we have the honor of announcing the 1958 Springfield High School "Queen Of Your Dreams."

MISSY goes to her purse to get out the prom ballot.

SUZY: The "Queen of your Dreams." That's the Prom Queen.

CINDY LOU: They already know that, do you think?

BETTY JEAN: The Prom Queen gets to pick her own King this year, so make sure you vote.

> *BETTY JEAN points to herself, mouthing "for me."*

CINDY LOU: Of course they'll vote, do you think? *(To Betty Jean)* I hope you win. *(To Suzy)* I hope you win.

> *There is a beat where CINDY LOU is waiting for the response.*

BETTY JEAN & SUZY *(unenthusiastically to Cindy Lou)*: I hope you win.

CINDY LOU *(seemingly touched)*: Thank you.

> *MISSY crosses back front, reading from the ballot.*

MISSY: There are five candidates for this year's Prom Queen.

> *MISSY gestures to each girl as announced.*

Betty Jean Reynolds.

> *BETTY JEAN waves.*

BETTY JEAN: And today's my birthday!

CINDY LOU: No sympathy votes.

MISSY: Cindy Lou Huffington.

> *CINDY LOU steps forward and waves.*

Suzy Simpson.

> *SUZY is turned US, bum in the air, fixing her shoe.*

Missy Miller, oh, that's me.

> *MISSY acknowledges herself.*

And Judy Carter.

> *MISSY crosses back to her purse to get the Student Handbook.*

CINDY LOU: Judy Carter?

BETTY JEAN: You know, Judy Carter. From Miss McPherson's Homeroom Class.

> *CINDY LOU still can't place her.*

With the mole!

> *BETTY JEAN illustrates her mole. CINDY LOU remembers.*

CINDY LOU: Oh—!

> *BETTY JEAN, CINDY LOU, and SUZY all illustrate their own versions of Judy's mole.*
>
> *MISSY crosses back to the microphone, and turns to get the girls' attention.*

MISSY *(to Betty Jean, Cindy Lou & Suzy)*: Girls— Eyes!

> *They all look at MISSY, and then MISSY turns back out to the audience.*

Judy Carter will be represented in absentia tonight due to a pre-existing appointment verified by the school nurse.

> *She holds up an excuse slip to show the audience.*

CINDY LOU *(to Betty Jean and Suzy)*: That's not really fair. I think you should be present to win, do you think?

> *CINDY LOU looks to SUZY, who makes an "I don't know" noise.*
>
> *MISSY reads from the student handbook.*

MISSY: According to the official student handbook, the "Queen Of Your Dreams" should be someone with poise, talent, elegance, and great school spirit.

> *BETTY JEAN races down front and performs a cartwheel, ending with her chipmunk face.*

BETTY JEAN: Go Chipmunks!

> *BETTY JEAN, SUZY, and CINDY LOU all get ballots.*

MISSY *(holding up a sample ballot)*: Suzy and I mimeographed the ballots.

> *All hold up ballots, sniff them and react.*

You should have all received one with your super senior prom program when you came in. Did you all receive a ballot? Hold them up, hold them up, hold them up...

> *MISSY and others (by example) encourage audience to "flutter" their ballots in the air.*

Thank you. Now put them away, put them away! We'll make an announcement when it's time to vote— so don't vote yet!

> *MISSY crosses back to return the items to her purse, sniffing the ballot again as she crosses.*

SUZY *(holding up the crown)*: And look what the Prom Queen gets!

> *CINDY LOU takes the crown.*

CINDY LOU *(posing with the crown)*: This is for the "Queen Of Your Dreams." *(Talking to the crown)* I'll see you later.

> *CINDY LOU kisses the crown. SUZY grabs it back.*

SUZY: Give it...!

MISSY: Tonight's honorary judge and official ballot counter is Miss McPherson. Merci. Merci, very much.

> *SUZY holds up the pillow with the Dream Catcher.*

SUZY: Missy...!

MISSY: It's time for the Dream Catcher.

> *The Dream Catcher is treated with reverence throughout. MISSY takes it from the pillow.*

Cindy Lou...?

CINDY LOU: We'll each get the chance to dedicate a song to our very own "dream lover" tonight. This marvelous Dream Catcher...

BETTY JEAN: Cootie catcher.

CINDY LOU: Cootie catcher.

MISSY: Dream Catcher!!

CINDY LOU: Dream Catcher.

> *CINDY LOU pinches BETTY JEAN on the arm.*

This marvelous Dream Catcher will decide who sings next.

SUZY: Missy made it.

> *MISSY proudly displays it out front.*

MISSY: I made it.

> *MISSY holds it up, ready to begin.*

Let's catch a dream.

> *They all gather around MISSY.*

ALL *(reverently)*: Let's catch a dream.

> *MISSY operates the Dream Catcher as they chant.*

L-O-V-E-That-Spells-Love!

> *CINDY LOU reaches over to lift the flap of the Dream Catcher, and MISSY reads the name.*

MISSY: Suzy's first!

> *SUZY squeals, hands the pillow to CINDY LOU, and jumps off the front of the platform toward the microphone. MISSY chastises her.*

Suzy...! Use the steps.

SUZY: Oh, sorry.

> *SUZY steps back up the front, turns, and leaps over the steps.*
>
> *She moves the microphone to her spot stage left, and then puts her gum on the microphone.*

Well, I'm sure you can all guess who my song is for, since I just got pinned last month!

> *The others squeal. SUZY giggles.*

SUZY (CONT'D): My song is for a very special boy—

> *She shows Ritchie's class ring, which she wears on a chain around her neck.*

—my date for the prom, Ritchie Stevens. I love you, Ritchie!!

> *As she waves to him, the lights flash.*

SONG #6: *STUPID CUPID*

> *(Singing)*

STUPID CUPID YOU'RE A REAL MEAN GUY
I'D LIKE TO CLIP YOUR WINGS SO YOU CAN'T FLY
I'M IN LOVE AND THAT'S A CRYING SHAME
AND I KNOW THAT YOU'RE THE ONE TO BLAME
HEY, HEY, SET ME FREE
STUPID CUPID, STOP PICKING ON ME!

I CAN'T DO MY HOMEWORK AND I CAN'T THINK STRAIGHT
I MEET HIM EV'RY MORNING ABOUT HALF PAST EIGHT
I'M ACTING LIKE A LOVESICK FOOL
YOU'VE EVEN GOT ME CARRYING HIS BOOKS TO SCHOOL
HEY, HEY, SET ME FREE
STUPID CUPID, STOP PICKING ON ME!

YOU MIXED ME UP BUT GOOD
RIGHT FROM THE VERY START
HEY GO PLAY ROBIN HOOD
WITH SOMEBODY ELSE'S HEART

YOU'VE GOT ME JUMPIN' LIKE A CRAZY CLOWN
AND I DON'T FEATURE WHAT YOU'RE PUTTIN' DOWN
SINCE I KISSED HIS LOVIN' LIPS OF WINE
THE THING THAT BOTHERS ME IS THAT I LIKE IT FINE
HEY, HEY, SET ME FREE
STUPID CUPID, STOP PICKING ON ME!

HEY, HEY, SET ME FREE
STUPID CUPID, STOP PICKING ON ME!

> *Applause.*

> *(Speaking)*

I love you Ritchie!

> *SUZY waves, the lights flash.*

MISSY: Suzy!

> *The lights restore. MISSY hands the Dream Catcher to SUZY.*

> *BETTY JEAN and CINDY LOU are playing with each other and chattering, not paying attention.*

Attention, eyes...!

SUZY *(with the Dream Catcher)*: Let's catch a dream.

ALL *(reverently)*: Let's catch a dream. *(Excitedly, as Suzy operates the Dream Cathcer)* L-O-V-E-That-Spells-Love!

> *BETTY JEAN reaches, but CINDY LOU slaps her hand and lifts the flap herself.*

SUZY: It's Betty Jean's turn!

SONG #7: LIPSTICK ON YOUR COLLAR

> *BETTY JEAN crosses down front, grabs the microphone, and crosses stage right.*

BETTY JEAN: Okay. Okay. Okay. Okay. Okay. Okay. This song is for my boyfriend, Johnny.

> *She points out to him, way in the back.*

(Singing)
WHEN YOU LEFT ME ALL ALONE
AT THE RECORD HOP
TOLD ME YOU WERE GOIN' OUT
FOR A SODA POP
YOU WERE GONE FOR QUITE A WHILE
HALF AN HOUR OR MORE
YOU CAME BACK, AND MAN OH MAN
THIS IS WHAT I SAW

LIPSTICK ON YOUR COLLAR
TOLD A TALE ON YOU
LIPSTICK ON YOUR COLLAR
SAID YOU WERE UNTRUE
BET YOUR BOTTOM DOLLAR
YOU AND I ARE THROUGH
'CAUSE LIPSTICK ON YOUR COLLAR
TOLD A TALE ON YOU

CINDY LOU, MISSY & SUZY:
> NYAH NYAH NYAH NYAH NYAH NYAH
> NYAH NYAH NYAH NYAH NYAH NYAH

BETTY JEAN:
> YOU SAID IT BELONGED TO ME
> MADE ME STOP AND THINK
> THEN I NOTICED YOURS WAS RED
> MINE WAS BABY PINK
> WHO WALKED IN BUT CINDY LOU
> LIPSTICK ALL A MESS
> WERE YOU SMOOCHING MY BEST FRIEND?
> GUESS THE ANSWER'S YES
>
> LIPSTICK ON YOUR COLLAR
> TOLD A TALE ON YOU
> LIPSTICK ON YOUR COLLAR
> SAID YOU WERE UNTRUE
> BET YOUR BOTTOM DOLLAR
> YOU AND I ARE THROUGH
> 'CAUSE LIPSTICK ON YOUR COLLAR
> TOLD A TALE ON YOU, BOY
> TOLD A TALE ON YOU, MAN
> TOLD A TALE ON

BETTY JEAN, MISSY & SUZY:
> YOU!

> *They all point accusingly at CINDY LOU.*

> *Applause.*

> *SUZY picks up the Dream Catcher.*

BETTY JEAN: I can't believe it— you were smackin' on Johnny behind my back!

CINDY LOU: Obviously you weren't keeping him happy.

BETTY JEAN: Obviously you're keeping all the boys happy.

MISSY & SUZY *(quietly)*: Oooh.

CINDY LOU: And what is that supposed to mean, Betty Jean?!

BETTY JEAN: You know exactly what that means, you bi—...

> *She is about to swear, the girls gasp, and CINDY LOU backs up in surprise.*

—boyfriend stealer!!

> *MISSY and SUZY try to stop them from fighting. SUZY moves between them with the Dream Catcher.*

SUZY: Can't you stop fighting for one night?

MISSY: You'll ruin everything!

> *And with that, BETTY JEAN grabs the Dream Catcher from SUZY and angrily starts the chant.*

BETTY JEAN: L-O-V-E-

> *The OTHERS rush over with concerned reverence.*

ALL: That-Spells-Love!

> *CINDY LOU leans over, lifts the flap and reads the name before BETTY JEAN gets a chance to speak.*

CINDY LOU: It's my turn!

BETTY JEAN: I'm supposed to say that...!

SONG #8: LUCKY LIPS

> *CINDY LOU moves the microphone center, offering SUZY back her gum, which is still on the mic.*

CINDY LOU: Suzy...!

SUZY *(taking the gum back)*: Sorry.

CINDY LOU: This is for...

> *She looks out back toward Johnny.*

...well, you know who you are!

> *(Singing)*
> WHEN I WAS JUST A LITTLE GIRL
> WITH LONG AND SILKY CURLS
> MY MOMMA TOLD ME, "HONEY
> YOU'VE GOT MORE THAN OTHER GIRLS
>
> NOW YOU KNOW YOU ARE GOOD LOOKIN'
> AND YOU'LL SOON WEAR DIAMOND CLIPS
> AND YOU'LL NEVER HAVE TO WORRY
> 'CUZ YOU'VE GOT LUCKY LIPS"

ALL:
> LUCKY LIPS ARE ALWAYS KISSIN'
> LUCKY LIPS ARE NEVER BLUE
> LUCKY LIPS WILL ALWAYS FIND A
> PAIR OF LIPS THAT WILL BE TRUE

CINDY LOU:
> I DON'T NEED A FOUR-LEAF CLOVER
> RABBIT'S FOOT OR GOOD LUCK CHARMS

CINDY LOU (CONT'D):
    WITH LUCKY LIPS I'LL ALWAYS HAVE
    A FELLA IN MY ARMS
BETTY JEAN, MISSY & SUZY:
    WITH LUCKY LIPS SHE'LL ALWAYS HAVE
    A FELLA IN HER ARMS

> *MISSY gets out a tambourine and accompanies the following.*

CINDY LOU:
    I NEVER GET HEARTBROKEN
    NO I'LL NEVER GET THE BLUES
    AND IF I PLAY THAT GAME OF LOVE
    I KNOW I JUST CAN'T LOSE
    WHEN THEY SPIN THAT WHEEL OF FORTUNE
    ALL I DO IS KISS MY CHIPS
    AND I KNOW I PICKED A WINNER
    'CUZ I'VE GOT LUCKY LIPS

> *BETTY JEAN grabs the tambourine and plays vigorously, getting louder and louder, disturbing CINDY LOU's song.*

ALL:
    LUCKY LIPS ARE ALWAYS KISSIN'
    LUCKY LIPS ARE NEVER BLUE
    LUCKY LIPS WILL ALWAYS FIND A
    PAIR OF LIPS THAT WILL BE TRUE
CINDY LOU:
    I DON'T NEED A FOUR-LEAF CLOVER
    RABBIT'S FOOT OR GOOD LUCK CHARMS

> *CINDY LOU grabs the tambourine from BETTY JEAN.*

    WITH LUCKY LIPS I'LL ALWAYS HAVE
    YOUR JOHNNY IN MY ARMS
BETTY JEAN: What? What did you say...?!

> *MISSY and SUZY grab BETTY JEAN to keep her from attacking CINDY LOU.*

MISSY, SUZY:
    WITH LUCKY LIPS SHE'LL ALWAYS HAVE
    YOUR JOHNNY...
MISSY: I'm sorry...

SUZY: She said it!

CINDY LOU:
    WITH LUCKY LIPS I'LL ALWAYS HAVE
    A FELLA IN MY ARMS!

> *Applause.*

> *MISSY moves to the stage left punchbowl, nervous that her turn to sing is next. SUZY gets the Dream Catcher. CINDY LOU and BETTY JEAN square off stage right.*

BETTY JEAN: Lucky lips...! Of all the boys you could have, did you have to steal mine? You're supposed to be my best friend!

> *CINDY LOU sticks her tongue out at BETTY JEAN, making a noise.*

Cindy Lou, you're really cruisin' for a bruisin'!

CINDY LOU: Oh yeah? Why don't you just D.D.T.— Drop Dead Twice.

BETTY JEAN: What? And look like you?!

> *BETTY JEAN makes a face, and SUZY rushes over to stop the fight.*

SUZY: Betty Jean! Don't...!

BETTY: She's been asking for it all night long!

CINDY LOU: Oh why don't you take a long walk off a short pier?

BETTY JEAN: Why don't you take a short walk... into the boys' locker Room!!

> *BETTY JEAN shoves CINDY LOU into the boys' locker room, offstage right.*

SUZY: Betty Jean! No!!

> *CINDY LOU races back on to fight with BETTY JEAN. They both square off, fists in the air, then proceed with a girly "slap-fight."*

> *SUZY uses the Dream Catcher phrase to stop them.*

Hey— L-O-V-E-That-Spells-Love!

> *There is a moment of uncertainty. CINDY LOU holds out her pinky, and BETTY JEAN hooks it with hers, repeating a pinky promise:*

BETTY JEAN & CINDY LOU: Best friends forever, boop!

> *BETTY JEAN and CINDY LOU grab hands and giggle together once again.*

SUZY: Girls, Eyes— It's Missy's turn!

SONG #9: SECRET LOVE

> *SUZY crosses to MISSY, who is hiding at the refreshment table left.*

Missy... it's your turn! My golly...

> *SUZY brings MISSY to the center microphone.*

SUZY (CONT'D): You look pretty.

MISSY: Thank you.

SUZY: Be marvelous!

MISSY: I'll try.

> *SUZY, CINDY LOU, and BETTY JEAN twirl in their dresses and sit on the steps of the platform.*
>
> *MISSY sings timidly at first, always careful not to look at Mr. Lee.*

(Singing)
ONCE I HAD A SECRET LOVE
THAT LIVED WITHIN THE HEART OF ME
ALL TOO SOON MY SECRET LOVE
BECAME IMPATIENT TO BE FREE

SO I TOLD A FRIENDLY STAR
THE WAY THAT DREAMERS OFTEN DO
JUST HOW WONDERFUL YOU ARE
AND WHY I'M SO IN LOVE WITH YOU

NOW I SHOUT IT FROM THE HIGHEST HILLS
EVEN TOLD THE GOLDEN DAFFODILS
AT LAST MY HEART'S AN OPEN DOOR
AND MY SECRET LOVE'S NO SECRET ANYMORE

> *MISSY curtseys, and runs back to the chalkboard.*
>
> *BETTY JEAN, CINDY LOU, and SUZY rise and move their mics as they talk to each other.*

SUZY: Missy's had a secret crush all year long. Now we finally get to find out who it is!

CINDY LOU: Tell us who it is!

BETTY JEAN: Yeah— who's your secret love?

> *MISSY jumps back and "presents" the name she's written in the heart on the chalkboard: Mr. Lee.*

SONG #10: MAN OF MY DREAMS MEDLEY:

[MR. LEE]

MISSY:
ONE, TWO, THREE

BETTY JEAN, CINDY LOU & SUZY *(to each other, surprised)*:
    HEY
MISSY:
    LOOK AT MR. LEE

    THREE, FOUR, FIVE
BETTY JEAN, CINDY LOU & SUZY *(knowingly, to Mr. Lee)*:
    HEY
MISSY:
    LOOK AT HIM JIVE

    MR. LEE, MR. LEE
MISSY & BETTY JEAN:
    HO! MR. LEE, MR. LEE, MR. LEE
MISSY, BETTY JEAN & SUZY:
    HO! MR. LEE, MR. LEE, MR. LEE
ALL:
    HO! MR. LEE, MR. LEE
MISSY:
    I MET MY SWEETIE

    HIS NAME IS MR. LEE

    I MET MY SWEETIE

    HIS NAME IS MR. LEE

    HE'S THE HANDSOMEST SWEETIE

    THAT YOU EVER DID SEE

    MY HEART IS ACHIN'

    FOR YOU MR. LEE

    MY HEART IS ACHIN'

    FOR YOU MR. LEE

    'CAUSE I LOVE YOU SO

    AND I'LL NEVER LET YOU GO
ALL:
    ONE, TWO, THREE— HEY!

    LOOK AT MR. LEE

    THREE, FOUR, FIVE— HEY!

    LOOK AT HIM JIVE
MISSY:
    MR. LEE, MR. LEE
MISSY & BETTY JEAN:
    HO! MR. LEE, MR. LEE, MR. LEE
MISSY, BETTY JEAN & SUZY:
    HO! MR. LEE, MR. LEE, MR. LEE

ALL:

HO! MR. LEE MR. LEE

MISSY stares at Mr. Lee as they sing.

SUZY:

HERE COMES MR. LEE

HE'S CALLING FOR ME

CINDY LOU:

HERE COMES MR. LEE

HE'S CALLING FOR ME

BETTY JEAN:

HE'S MY LOVER BOY

LET'S JUMP FOR JOY

MISSY:

COME ON MR. LEE

AND DO YOUR STUFF

COME ON MR. LEE

AND DO YOUR STUFF

'CAUSE YOU'RE GONNA BE MINE

'TIL THE END OF TIME

ALL:

ONE, TWO, THREE— HEY!

LOOK AT MR. LEE

THREE, FOUR, FIVE

LOOK AT HIM JIVE

MR. LEE, MR. LEE, HO! MR. LEE

MR. LEE, MR. LEE, HO! MR. LEE

MR. LEE, MR. LEE, HO! MR. LEE

MR. LEE

The girls promenade in front of Mr. Lee.

[BORN TOO LATE]

BORN TOO LATE FOR YOU TO NOTICE ME

TO YOU, I'M JUST A KID THAT YOU WON'T DATE

WHY WAS I BORN TOO LATE?

BORN TOO LATE TO HAVE A CHANCE TO WIN

YOUR LOVE, OH WHY, OH WHY WAS IT MY FATE

TO BE BORN TOO LATE?

MISSY takes off her glasses, blinking furiously, and tries to sing toward the general vicinity of Mr. Lee.

MISSY:
I SEE YOU WALK WITH ANOTHER
I WISH IT COULD BE ME
I LONG TO HOLD YOU AND KISS YOU

BETTY JEAN instructs MISSY to put on her glasses.

BETTY JEAN: Put your glasses on!

MISSY puts on her glasses, and apologizes profusely to whom she was singing over the next sung line.

MISSY: I'm sorry, Ma'am! I thought you were Mr. Lee!

BETTY JEAN, CINDY LOU & SUZY:
BUT I KNOW IT NEVER CAN BE

BETTY JEAN and SUZY go into audience to get Mr. Lee. CINDY LOU gets a stool and places it center of the platform.

FOR I WAS
BORN TOO LATE FOR YOU TO CARE NOW
MY HEART CRIES, OH WHY, OH WHY WAS IT MY FATE?
TO BE BORN TOO LATE?

SUZY *(to Missy)*: Missy... you're missin' it!

BETTY JEAN brings Mr. Lee onto the stage. They seat him on the stool.

[TEACHER'S PET]

MISSY:
TEACHER'S PET, I WANNA BE
TEACHER'S PET, I WANNA BE
HUDDLED, AND CUDDLED
AS CLOSE TO YOU AS I CAN GET
BETTY JEAN, CINDY LOU & SUZY:
THAT'S THE LESSON WE'RE GUESSIN' YOU'RE BEST IN
BETTY JEAN:
TEACHER'S PRIDE, I WANNA BE
TEACHER'S PRIDE, I WANNA BE
DATED, AND RATED
THE ONE MOST LIKELY AT YOUR SIDE
CINDY LOU, MISSY & SUZY:
SHE'S GOT A BURNIN' YEARNIN' TO LEARN
CINDY LOU:
I WANNA LEARN ALL YOUR LIPS CAN TEACH ME
ONE KISS WILL DO AT THE START

SUZY:
I'M SURE WITH A LITTLE HOMEWORK

> *SUZY takes his arm and places it around her waist, keeping his hand hidden.*

I'LL GRADUATE TO YOUR...

> *She reacts like he goosed her, holding her backside.*

(Speaking)

Mr. Lee!

ALL:
TEACHER'S PET, WE WANNA BE
TEACHER'S PET, WE WANNA BE
HUDDLED, AND CUDDLED
AS CLOSE TO YOU AS WE CAN GET
THAT'S THE LESSON WE'RE GUESSIN' YOU'RE BEST IN

MISSY:
TEACHER'S PET

BETTY JEAN, CINDY LOU & SUZY:
SHE LOVES THE TEACHER

MISSY:
I WANNA BE TEACHER'S PET
I WANNA TAKE HOME A DIPLOMA
AND SHOW MA THAT YOU LOVE ME TOO
SO I CAN BE TEACHER'S PET
LONG AFTER SCHOOL IS THROUGH

ALL:
TEACHER, TEACHER, WE LOVE YOU

> *MISSY leads everyone in vigorous applause as BETTY JEAN escorts Mr. Lee to his seat.*

SOUND: BUZZER

BETTY JEAN: Stop, drop and roll!

> *CINDY LOU, MISSY and SUZY all drop to the floor and tuck and roll, showing their ruffled panties.*
>
> *BETTY JEAN is very pleased with herself.*

Yes!

MUFFLED TEACHER (V.O.): It is now time for the talent portion of the 1958 Springfield High School "Queen Of Your Dreams" campaign.

> *The girls all understand this immediately, and rise. BETTY JEAN brings a microphone over to MISSY.*

MISSY: It's almost time to vote for the "Queen Of Your Dreams!"

SUZY: That's the prom queen!

MISSY: But first we'll have the personal talent presentation before you make your final choice for the "Queen Of Your Dreams."

SUZY: That's the prom queen!

MISSY: In an ongoing effort to keep the evening moving along, the rules committee has decided that the talent portion of the Queen campaign will be 30 seconds long, to be performed simultaneously by each Queen nominee. As announced earlier, Judy Carter is excused from tonight's talent presentation due to her appointment with the girl doctor.

> *MISSY moves her mic back, and the girls get into "place," ready to begin.*

Are we all ready?

BETTY JEAN, CINDY LOU & SUZY: Yes...!

MISSY: Let the presentation begin!

QUEEN CAMPAIGN MUSIC

> *CINDY LOU poses. A lot.*
>
> *MISSY sings some vocal warm-ups, and then repeatedly hits her "money note."*
>
> *SUZY does the Lemon Twist while blowing bubble-gum bubbles.*
>
> *BETTY JEAN sets up a flaming baton routine, bringing out a bucket, a baton, a gas can and a zippo lighter. After she pours gas onto the ends of the baton, she flips open the zippo and...*

> **SOUND: BUZZER**

BETTY JEAN: What?!

MUSICAL "TADA" BUTTON

> *CINDY LOU, MISSY, and SUZY each curtsey, while BETTY JEAN is baffled that she didn't get to finish her routine.*

CINDY LOU, MISSY & SUZY: Thank you!

BETTY JEAN: No!!

MUFFLED TEACHER (V.O.): It is now time to vote for the "Queen Of Your Dreams."

BETTY JEAN: But I didn't even get to light my stick!

> *BETTY JEAN begins to clean up, while SUZY and CINDY LOU begin giving instructions to the audience.*

MISSY tries to get everyone's attention.

MISSY: Eyes. Attention everyone— eyes!! There are some important rules that must be addressed before you vote... wait, please... you must all hear the rules from the committee...

MISSY shouts.

I must have your eyes!!!

All stop and watch MISSY.

Thank you. When voting, please use the special number two pencils provided by Miss McPherson's Thursday morning golf class. When you're finished with your pencils, do not drop them onto the gym floor. I repeat, do not drop your pencils onto the floor. This is considered littering and will not be tolerated.

BETTY JEAN tosses a pencil at MISSY's feet.

Betty Jean!

BETTY JEAN points to an audience member.

BETTY JEAN: She did it!

MISSY and SUZY gasp toward the person.

MISSY *(to audience member)*: Litter-er. *(Back to audience in general)* You will hand in your pencils after the prom. After the prom. When you are finished voting, please pass your ballots over to the aisle. Over to the aisle. And everyone PLEASE keep your eyes on your own papers. Nobody likes a "Peter, Peter, Pumpkin Cheater." And now, everyone get out your ballots and circle your choice for the Marvelous "Queen of your Dreams."

SUZY: That's the prom queen!

SONG #11: BALLOT MUSIC

The girls all move to positions in the house to help collect the ballots. During the ballot collection, BETTY JEAN and CINDY LOU remind patrons who to vote for.

[SUZY takes the ENVELOPE to Miss McPherson, quietly explaining that someone will be asking for it after the next song. She also informs her that she'll have some ballots given to her and be asked to count them— and it's not necessary to count them.]

When the ballots are collected, everyone returns to the stage. They pass the ballots to MISSY.

MISSY: I think we're ready— Attention everyone, eyes!

MISSY crosses toward Miss McPherson.

Miss McPherson, count these! Hurry!!!

MISSY tosses them all into Miss McPherson's lap.

CINDY LOU: Well, the entertainment portion of our super senior prom has come to an end.

BETTY JEAN: We'd like to give a special merci and boup-coo to Miss McPherson and her French class for helping Missy with the terrific decorations.

They quickly repeat their French words as before.

CINDY LOU: Oui, oui, oui.

MISSY: Oh, merci very much.

SUZY: Croissant. *(Stepping to the mic)* We should also thank Billy Ray Patton for being a butthead so that we could be here.

The girls all react affirmatively.

BETTY JEAN: Ha! Butthead!

BETTY JEAN and SUZY giggle together.

MISSY: Betty Jean! And a super big thank you to our super Chipmunk Leader, Mr. Lee.

ALL: Thank you Mr. Lee!

They make their chipmunk faces to him.

SONG #12: GOODNIGHT AND GOODBYE MEDLEY:

[SINCERELY]

They all move up to the platform.

SUZY *(to Missy as they cross up)*: You love him. You're gonna marry him!

MISSY: Stop it— you're embarrassing me!

CINDY LOU *(to audience)*: We hope all of your Marvelous Dreams come true.

She stares at Miss McPherson.

I'm sure mine will.

ALL:
SINCERELY, OH YES, SINCERELY
'CAUSE I LOVE YOU SO DEARLY
PLEASE SAY YOU'LL BE MINE

MISSY *(giving dance instructions)*: Down, up.

ALL:
SINCERELY, OH YOU KNOW HOW I LOVE YOU
I'LL DO ANYTHING FOR YOU
PLEASE SAY YOU'LL BE MINE

MISSY: Down, up.

BETTY JEAN:
OH LORD, WON'T YOU TELL ME WHY
I LOVE THAT FELLOW SO

ALL:
HE DOESN'T WANT ME

BETTY JEAN:
BUT I'LL NEVER, NEVER, NEVER, NEVER

ALL:
LET HIM GO
SINCERELY, OH YOU KNOW HOW I LOVE YOU
I'LL DO ANYTHING FOR YOU
PLEASE SAY YOU'LL BE MINE

MISSY: Down, and up.

[GOODNIGHT SWEETHEART]

BETTY JEAN: I'd like to dedicate this to Johnny.

CINDY LOU: Me too.

> *BETTY JEAN becomes distraught as the song progresses.*

ALL:
GOODNIGHT SWEETHEART, WELL IT'S TIME TO GO
GOODNIGHT SWEETHEART, WELL IT'S TIME TO GO
I HATE TO LEAVE YOU BUT I REALLY MUST SAY
GOODNIGHT SWEETHEART, GOODNIGHT

> *CINDY LOU blows a kiss to Johnny, giggling, making sure BETTY JEAN witnesses it all.*

ALL:
GOODNIGHT SWEETHEART, WELL IT'S TIME TO GO

CINDY LOU: Goodnight, Johnny!

> *This destroys BETTY JEAN, who repairs to the stage right refreshment table for consolation.*

CINDY LOU, MISSY & SUZY:
GOODNIGHT SWEETHEART, WELL IT'S TIME TO GO
I HATE TO LEAVE YOU BUT I REALLY MUST SAY
GOODNIGHT SWEETHEART, GOODNIGHT

> *SUZY crosses to BETTY JEAN. They have a silent yet animated discussion.*

CINDY LOU & MISSY:
WELL IT'S THREE O'CLOCK IN THE MORNIN'
BABY, I JUST CAN'T TREAT YOU RIGHT

MISSY also crosses to BETTY JEAN. CINDY LOU then makes the best of her new solo section.

During the "discussion" at the refreshment table, we hear BETTY JEAN protesting: "But it's my birthday!"

CINDY LOU:

OH I HATE TO LEAVE YOU BABY

I DON'T MEAN MAYBE

BECAUSE I LOVE YOU

MISSY and SUZY get BETTY JEAN to rejoin the group.

ALL:

SO

BETTY JEAN shoves CINDY LOU off of the platform. CINDY LOU poses to recover.

GOODNIGHT SWEETHEART, WELL IT'S TIME TO GO

CINDY LOU comes back onto the platform.

GOODNIGHT SWEETHEART, WELL IT'S TIME TO GO

CINDY LOU covers BETTY JEAN's face with her hand during the choreography.

I HATE TO LEAVE YOU, BUT I REALLY MUST SAY

BETTY JEAN pinches CINDY LOU in the arm, as CINDY LOU did to her earlier.

CINDY LOU: Ow, ow, ow, ow, ow, ow... Betty Jean!!

ALL:

GOODNIGHT SWEETHEART, GOODNIGHT

BETTY JEAN moves her microphone forward.

BETTY JEAN:

OH LORD, WON'T YOU TELL ME WHY

I LOVE THAT FELLOW SO?

HE DOESN'T WANT ME

BUT I'LL NEVER, NEVER, NEVER, NEVER

LET HIM GO

CINDY LOU brings her microphone forward to line up with BETTY JEAN.

CINDY LOU:

NO, I'LL NEVER, NEVER, NEVER, NEVER

ALL:

LET HIM GO

CINDY LOU and BETTY JEAN now vie for Johnny's attention.

SINCERELY

> *MISSY moves her microphone up, followed by SUZY.*

ALL (CONT'D):
OH YOU KNOW HOW I LOVE YOU

> *BETTY JEAN moves her microphone up again, followed by CINDY LOU.*

I'LL DO ANYTHING FOR YOU

> *MISSY moves her microphone up again, followed by SUZY.*

PLEASE SAY YOU'LL BE MINE

> *BETTY JEAN moves forward one last time.*

BETTY JEAN:
PLEASE SAY YOU'LL BE...

SOUND: BUZZER

> *BETTY JEAN is interrupted by the school buzzer, and the song stops abruptly.*
>
> *BETTY JEAN vocally protests in spurts throughout the buzzer and announcement.*

What?! No fair!!

MUFFLED TEACHER (V.O.): It is now time to announce the "Queen of Your Dreams!"

SUZY: Oh my golly!

MISSY: It's time to announce the "Queen Of Your Dreams!"

SUZY: That's the Prom Queen!

> *They all come down front, CINDY LOU preparing to receive her crown.*

BETTY JEAN: No, no, no! I was singing to Johnny! My first song didn't count...!

CINDY LOU: Oh, will you please just get the envelope?

> *BETTY JEAN imitates CINDY LOU.*

BETTY JEAN: Oh, will you please just get the envelope?

> *MISSY demands her attention.*

MISSY: Betty Jean! Marvelous!!

> *BETTY JEAN makes her marvelous pose with a strained smile. She then moves down to Miss McPherson, with attitude.*

BETTY JEAN: Miss McPherson— give me the damn envelope!

MISSY: Betty Jean!!

> *BETTY JEAN makes a slight adjustment.*

BETTY JEAN: Give me the damn envelope, s'il vous plaît.

She brings the envelope back onstage. She holds it in front of CINDY LOU.

BETTY JEAN (CONT'D): You open it.

CINDY LOU: Well I can't open it, do you think?

SUZY takes the envelope, giggling.

MISSY: Oh, for heaven's sake— I'll open it!

MISSY grabs the envelope from SUZY.

This year's "Queen Of Your Dreams" is...

SOIND: DRUM ROLL

MISSY opens the envelope and pulls out the paper and reads.

I can't believe it! It's Suzy Simpson!

CINDY LOU: What?!

BETTY JEAN: Yes!!

12A. BALLOT OPENING FANFARE

BETTY JEAN gets the audience to applaud.

The lights flash wildly, and SUZY swallows her gum.

MISSY: Oh!!! She swallowed her gum!

She struggles as MISSY fans the envelope in her face.

BETTY JEAN: She swallowed her gum! She swallowed her gum! Cindy Lou— do something!

CINDY LOU comes up from behind and slaps SUZY on the back. SUZY spits out the gum. She picks it up and holds it.

SUZY (excited at winning): Wow!

SUZY puts the gum back in her mouth.

MISSY and BETTY JEAN help SUZY on with the sash, while CINDY LOU holds and covets the crown.

BETTY JEAN finally rips the crown out of CINDY LOU's hands and hands it to SUZY.

BETTY JEAN: Here's your hat!

SUZY puts the crown on. Throughout the above, SUZY repeats "Wow!"

MISSY: And now Suzy gets to pick her Prom King! Three questions...

BETTY JEAN, CINDY LOU & MISSY: Three questions!

BETTY JEAN: Is he someone you love?

SUZY: Yes!

MISSY: Is he someone we know?

SUZY: Yes!

CINDY LOU: Is he here tonight?

SUZY: You know who it is! It's Ritchie Stevens!!

She waves to Ritchie and the stage goes dark.

BETTY JEAN, CINDY LOU & MISSY: Ritchie!

Lights restore.

SUZY: That's funny.

MISSY: Suzy— It's time for your spotlight song!

SONG #13: HOLD ME, THRILL ME, KISS ME

SUZY: Wow...!

The OTHERS move back onto the platform.

CINDY LOU lingers for a moment in the spotlight, mouthing the first few words.

(Singing)
HOLD ME, HOLD ME
NEVER LET ME GO UNTIL YOU'VE
TOLD ME, TOLD ME
WHAT I WANT TO KNOW AND THEN JUST

BETTY JEAN, CINDY LOU, and MISSY join in and sing back-ups throughout the song.

HOLD ME, HOLD ME
MAKE ME TELL YOU I'M IN LOVE WITH YOU

Ritchie flashes the lights. SUZY giggles.

THRILL ME, THRILL ME
WALK ME DOWN THE LANE
WHERE SHADOWS WILL BE

WE'LL BE
HIDING LOVERS JUST THE SAME AS
WE'LL BE—
WE'LL BE
WHEN YOU MAKE ME TELL YOU I LOVE YOU

THEY TOLD ME "BE SENSIBLE
WITH YOUR NEW LOVE

SUZY (CONT'D):
> DON'T BE FOOLED THINKING
> THIS IS THE LAST YOU'LL FIND"
> BUT THEY NEVER STOOD IN THE DARK
> WITH YOU LOVE
> WHEN YOU TAKE ME IN YOUR ARMS
> AND DRIVE ME
> SLOWLY OUT OF MY MIND
>
> KISS ME, KISS ME
> WHEN YOU DO I'LL KNOW
> THAT YOU WILL MISS ME
> MISS ME
> IF WE EVER SAY
> > *(Proudly toward Miss McPherson)*
> "ADIEU"
> > *(Back out to Ritchie)*
> SO KISS ME
> KISS ME
> MAKE ME TELL YOU I'M IN LOVE WITH YOU
> > *SUZY does a quick "wave & walk," and the OTHERS move down behind her.*
> KISS ME
> WHEN YOU DO I'LL KNOW
> THAT YOU WILL
> MISS ME, MISS ME
> IF WE EVER SAY "ADIEU"
> SO KISS ME, KISS ME
> MAKE ME TELL YOU I'M IN LOVE WITH YOU
>
> NO, NO, NEVER
> NO, NO NEVER LET ME GO
> NEVER, NEVER, NEVER LET ME GO
> NEVER, NEVER, NEVER
> LET ME GO—

ALL:
> NEVER, NEVER, NEVER
> LET ME GO

The lights flash repeatedly as the girls all gather around to congratulate SUZY.

CINDY LOU reaches out to touch the crown on SUZY's head as the lights fade.

END OF ACT I

ACT II

1968, SPRINGFIELD, USA.

It is now ten years later, and we are in the same high school gymnasium. The framed portrait of the president on the wall should now be Lyndon B. Johnson.

The gymnasium is now decorated for the Class of 1958's Ten-Year Reunion. On the tables are wine and champagne bottles and glasses.

After the lights go to black, we hear:

PRINCIPAL (V.O.): Class of '58, this is Principal Varney. Welcome back to Springfield High School and your Ten Year Reunion!

SONG #14: HEATWAVE

It really is marvelous to see so many familiar faces out there. We have a great program planned for you this evening. Back together for the first time in ten years—wow, can you believe it's been that long? Please welcome back your very own Marvelous Wonderettes!

> *Lights up as CINDY LOU, BETTY JEAN, and MISSY are revealed in their '60s outfits and hair.*
>
> *The backdrop has changed to a '60s design as well, with a banner reading "Class of 1958—Ten Year Reunion."*
>
> *The girls strut forward to their microphones.*

CINDY LOU:
WHENEVER I'M WITH HIM, SOMETHING INSIDE
STARTS TO BURNIN', AND I FILL WITH DESIRE
COULD IT BE A DEVIL IN ME
OR IS THIS THE WAY LOVE'S SUPPOSED TO BE?
IT'S LIKE A

BETTY JEAN, CINDY LOU & MISSY:
HEATWAVE

CINDY LOU:
BURNING IN MY HEART
I CAN'T KEEP FROM CRYING
IT'S TEARING ME APART

> *BETTY JEAN moves to the solo spot.*

BETTY JEAN:
WHENEVER HE CALLS MY NAME
SOFT, LOW, SWEET AND PLAIN
I FEEL, RIGHT THERE, I FEEL THAT BURNING FLAME

MISSY moves to the solo spot.

MISSY:
YES, HIGH BLOOD PRESSURE'S GOT A HOLD ON ME
OR IS THIS THE WAY LOVE'S SUPPOSED TO BE?
IT'S LIKE A

BETTY JEAN, CINDY LOU & MISSY:
HEATWAVE

MISSY:
BURNING IN MY HEART
I CAN'T KEEP FROM CRYING
IT'S TEARING ME APART

MISSY moves back, leaving the solo spot for SUZY, who is nowhere to be found.

(Speaking)

Where is she?

BETTY JEAN: I thought she was right behind you.

BETTY JEAN, CINDY LOU & MISSY:
HEY! HEATWAVE!

MISSY *(calling and running off-stage)*: Suzy!

SUZY *(from offstage)*: Just a minute...

CINDY LOU: She's probably tossing her cookies again...

BETTY JEAN & CINDY LOU:
HEATWAVE!

MISSY pushes SUZY onstage. SUZY is rushed and panting, carrying her boots. She is very pregnant. She hands her boots to MISSY and comes forward to the microphone.

SUZY:
SOMETIMES I STARE IN SPACE
TEARS ALL OVER MY FACE
I CAN'T EXPLAIN IT, DON'T UNDERSTAND IT
I AIN'T NEVER FELT LIKE THIS BEFORE
NOW THIS BURNING FEELING HAS ME ABLAZE
DON'T KNOW WHAT TO DO, MY HEAD'S IN A HAZE
IT'S LIKE A

ALL:
HEATWAVE

SUZY *(*simultaneous)*:
YEAH, YEAH, YEAH, YEAH, OH
YEAH, YEAH, YEAH, YEAH
OH
I FEEL IT BURNING
RIGHT HERE IN MY HEART

SUZY (CONT'D) (*simultaneous):
DON'T YOU KNOW IT'S LIKE A

BETTY JEAN, CINDY LOU & MISSY (*simultaneous, background):
YOU KNOW IT'S ALRIGHT GIRL
GO AHEAD GIRL
WELL IT'S ALRIGHT
AIN'T NOTHIN' BUT SOUL GIRL
DON'T PASS UP THIS CHANCE
IT'S TIME FOR A TRUE ROMANCE

> *SUZY goes and grabs a stool from near the refreshment stand. She drags it back to her spot and sits.*

ALL:
HEATWAVE
IT'S LIKE A HEATWAVE!

> *Applause.*

CINDY LOU (quickly to Suzy, during applause): Are you alright?

SUZY: It's okay— go ahead. I'll be alright.

> *SUZY puts the stool back before coming up on to the platform.*

CINDY LOU: Hi everyone! Welcome to our Ten Year Reunion! I'm Cynthia.

> *BETTY JEAN reacts, making fun of CINDY LOU's "new name."*

BETTY JEAN (to Çindy Lou): Ooh— Cynthia. (To audience) She's Cindy Lou and I'm B.J.

MISSY: I'm Missy.

> *SUZY gets in line with her microphone just in time.*

SUZY (out of breath): Suzy.

CINDY LOU: And we're...

ALL: The Marvelous Wonderettes! (They strike their pose with a noise) Hhmmm!

SONG #15: MR. SANDMAN REPRISE

> *They react to the happy memory of the music.*

> (Singing)
BUM, BUM, BUM, BUM, BUM, BUM, BUM, BUM
BUM, BUM, BUM, BUM, BUM

> *SUZY feels the baby kick. This should be a gentle kick, no cause for alarm.*

SUZY: Oh! Oh!

MISSY checks in with SUZY, who gestures that she's fine.

ALL:
BUM, BUM, BUM, BUM, BUM, BUM, BUM, BUM
BUM, BUM, BUM, BUM, BUM
MR. SANDMAN, BRING ME A DREAM
MAKE HIM THE CUTEST THAT I'VE EVER SEEN
GIVE HIM TWO LIPS LIKE ROSES IN CLOVER
THEN TELL HIM THAT HIS LONESOME NIGHTS ARE OVER

SANDMAN, I'M SO ALONE
DON'T HAVE NOBODY TO CALL MY OWN
PLEASE TURN ON YOUR MAGIC BEAM
MR. SANDMAN, BRING US A DREAM
SUZY:
MR. SANDMAN

RITCHIE'S VOICE (V.O.): What do you want now?!

SUZY breaks into tears and the song falls apart.

MISSY: I thought this might happen.

BETTY JEAN *(aside to Cindy Lou)*: Trouble in paradise.

CINDY LOU *(aside to Betty Jean)*: Are they still fighting?

MISSY *(to Cindy Lou & Betty Jean)*: Everything's alright. *(Out to audience)* Everything's alright. Suzy and Ritchie got married right after graduation. That's quite a long time, and right now they're just going through a little rough patch.

SUZY: Rough patch...

SUZY sobs once again.

MISSY: Betty Jean, cover.

MISSY gets a hanky from her purse for SUZY.

BETTY JEAN: When they were organizing this reunion, Mr. Lee asked us— well, asked Missy— if we could get our group back together.

CINDY LOU: Suzy and Missy still see each other all the time, but the rest of us hardly ever talk.

BETTY JEAN: Why don't we let Missy tell the story... *(Mocking her name again)* ...alright Cynthia?

CINDY LOU: Okay fine.

BETTY JEAN: Fine.

CINDY LOU: Fine!

BETTY JEAN: Fine!

MISSY (*quickly putting an end to the argument*): Fine. Well, one day, out of the blue, Mr. Lee asked me if we would perform again as a group. I knew we were all back in Springfield, so Suzy and I tracked everyone down, and here we are! (*She holds her hands up posing*) Ta da!

BETTY JEAN, CINDY LOU & SUZY (*mimicking the pose*): Ta da.

SUZY: Missy made our dresses again.

MISSY (*proudly, closely into mic*): Butterick's 5-9-2-7.

SUZY (*tugging at her dress*): She took our measurements a month ago.

MISSY: I'm sorry.

BETTY JEAN: And Ritchie is back running the lights.

SUZY: Hi Ritchie, honey.

> *There is no reaction.*

> *SUZY bursts into tears and crosses away.*

MISSY: I think we need the Dream Catcher!

> *MISSY gets her purse.*

BETTY JEAN: Dream Catcher?!

CINDY LOU: Oh wow. I haven't seen one of those since high school.

BETTY: Whataya bet it's the same one we had at the prom?

CINDY LOU: Do you think?

MISSY: Of course it's the same one. You know me—

> *CINDY LOU and BETTY JEAN chime in with MISSY. They speak together:*

BETTY JEAN & CINDY LOU: You save everything.

MISSY: I save everything.

> *They chuckle. MISSY rustles through her purse.*

BETTY JEAN: Can you believe she kept that Cootie Catcher all these years?

CINDY LOU: Dream Catcher.

BETTY JEAN: Cootie Catcher!

> *MISSY has become distraught.*

MISSY: It doesn't matter what it's called— I can't find it.

> *SUZY crosses toward MISSY.*

Suzy, I know I put it in here this morning...

> *She continues searching.*

SUZY: You told me you put it in there.

MISSY: But now it's gone.

SUZY: It's gone...?

SUZY sobs again. MISSY puts the purse down and brings SUZY back onto the platform.

MISSY: It's alright, Suzy. It doesn't matter. I'll just start first.

This brings SUZY back into the group.

SUZY: Okay. You start first. Three questions.

BETTY JEAN & CINDY LOU: Three questions?!

SUZY definitely wants to play.

SUZY: Three questions!

MISSY wants to keep SUZY involved.

MISSY *(to Betty Jean and Cindy Lou)*: Three questions!

SUZY: Are you in love?

MISSY: Yes.

CINDY LOU: Is he someone we know?

MISSY: Yes.

BETTY JEAN: Is he here tonight?

MISSY: Yes. And I've been keeping this a secret from everyone.

CINDY LOU: What?

BETTY JEAN: Who is it?

MISSY: I've been going out with Bill for the past five years.

CINDY LOU: Bill?

BETTY JEAN: Bill who?

MISSY: Mr. Lee.

BETTY JEAN & CINDY LOU: Mr. Lee?!

They all look at Mr. Lee.

MISSY: Oh c'mon girls. We were all in love with him. I just happen to be the only one to do anything about it.

CINDY LOU: Yeah, but how did you two...

MISSY: Well, before I started teaching full time at Maple Leaf Elementary, I was a substitute art teacher right here at Springfield High. Go Chipmunks!

ALL: Go Chipmunks!

They all make the chipmunk faces together.

MISSY: Well, Bill and I would see each other in the halls, and he always had a little wink in his eye for me. Finally, one night he asked me out for pizza. Then we sort of made it a regular thing— every Monday night, more pizza. Bill and I have been having pizza for the past five years. *(She takes her microphone and crosses down front center)* And now I have only one question:

SONG #16: IT'S IN HIS KISS/WEDDING BELL BLUES

MISSY (CONT'D):
DOES HE LOVE ME? I WANNA KNOW
HOW CAN I TELL IF HE LOVES ME SO?

> *SUZY, BETTY JEAN, and CINDY LOU bring their microphones
> down as well. SUZY joins MISSY center.*

IS IT IN HIS EYES?
SUZY:
OH NO, YOU'LL BE DECEIVED
MISSY:
IS IT IN HIS SIGHS?
SUZY:
OH NO, HE'LL MAKE BELIEVE
IF YOU WANNA KNOW
IF HE LOVES YOU SO
IT'S IN HIS KISS
BETTY JEAN & CINDY LOU:
THAT'S WHERE IT IS, OH YEAH
MISSY:
OR IS IT IN HIS FACE?
SUZY:
OH NO, THAT'S JUST HIS CHARMS
MISSY:
IN HIS WARM EMBRACE?
SUZY:
OH NO, THAT'S JUST HIS ARMS
IF YOU WANNA KNOW
IF HE LOVES YOU SO
IT'S IN HIS KISS
BETTY JEAN & CINDY LOU:
THAT'S WHERE IT IS, OH YEAH
SUZY:
OH, IT'S IN HIS KISS
BETTY JEAN & CINDY LOU:
THAT'S WHERE IT IS

> *SUZY pushes MISSY over toward the others.*

SUZY: Tell her, girls!
BETTY JEAN:
KISS HIM, AND SQUEEZE HIM TIGHT
CINDY LOU:
AND FIND OUT WHAT YOU WANNA KNOW

SUZY:
IF IT'S LOVE, IF IT REALLY IS

> *SUZY brings MISSY back center and joins the OTHERS stage right.*

BETTY JEAN, CINDY LOU & SUZY:
IT'S THERE IN HIS KISS

MISSY:
HOW 'BOUT THE WAY HE ACTS?

BETTY JEAN:
OH NO, THAT'S NOT THE WAY

CINDY LOU:
AND YOU'RE NOT LISTENING TO WHAT WE SAY

SUZY:
IF YOU WANNA KNOW

IF HE LOVES YOU SO

IT'S IN HIS KISS

BETTY JEAN & CINDY LOU:
THAT'S WHERE IT IS, OH YEAH

SUZY:
OH YEAH, IT'S IN HIS KISS

BETTY JEAN & CINDY LOU:
THAT'S WHERE IT IS

SUZY: Let's show her, girls.

> *A short dance break where the girls try to get MISSY to loosen up. They give her a few dance moves.*

CINDY LOU: And swim, swim.

MISSY *(repeating the dance stiffly)*: Swim, swim.

BETTY JEAN: Oh, c'mon— try this!

SUZY: You gotta loosen up, Missy!

> *MISSY tries.*

> *MISSY finally shimmies wildly and the OTHERS celebrate.*

MISSY:
BILL

I LOVE YOU SO, I ALWAYS WILL

I LOOK AT YOU AND YOU SEE THE PASSION EYES OF MAY

OH, BUT AM I EVER GONNA SEE MY WEDDING DAY?

OH, I WAS ON YOUR SIDE BILL

WHEN YOU WERE LOSIN'

I NEVER SCHEMED OR LIED, BILL

THERE'S BEEN NO FOOLIN'

MISSY (CONT'D):
BUT KISSES AND LOVE WON'T CARRY ME
UNTIL YOU MARRY ME BILL
I LOVE YOU SO, I ALWAYS WILL
AND IN YOUR VOICE I HEAR A CHOIR OF CAROUSELS
OH, BUT AM I EVER GONNA HEAR MY WEDDING BELLS?

I WAS THE ONE CAME RUNNING
WHEN YOU WERE LONELY
I HAVEN'T LIVED ONE DAY
NOT LOVIN' YOU ONLY
BUT KISSES AND LOVE WON'T CARRY ME
UNTIL YOU MARRY ME BILL
I LOVE YOU SO, I ALWAYS WILL
AND THOUGH DEVOTION RULES MY HEART
I TAKE NO BOWS
OH BUT BILL, YOU KNOW
I WANT TO TAKE MY WEDDING VOWS

COME ON BILL
YEAH, COME ON BILL
COME AND MARRY ME BILL
I'VE GOT THE WEDDING BELL BLUES
WHY WON'T YOU MARRY ME BILL?
COME ON AND MARRY ME BILL!

Applause.

CINDY LOU moves down front to MISSY.

CINDY LOU: Wait, wait, wait, wait, wait a minute, Missy. I think you might be getting carried away. That sounded a little like you were begging.

MISSY: I was begging.

CINDY LOU: Oh, no, no, no, no, no, no, no, no. Never beg.

SONG #17: YOU DON'T OWN ME

She turns to face Mr. Lee.

(Singing)
YOU DON'T OWN HER
SHE'S NOT JUST ONE OF YOUR MANY TOYS
YOU DON'T OWN HER
BE NICE, OR SHE MAY GO WITH OTHER BOYS

BETTY JEAN and SUZY join CINDY LOU down front.

BETTY JEAN, CINDY LOU & SUZY:
AND DON'T TELL HER WHAT TO DO
AND DON'T TELL HER WHAT TO SAY
AND PLEASE WHEN SHE GOES OUT WITH YOU
DON'T PUT HER ON DISPLAY

They each grab the microphone and sing at Mr. Lee.

BETTY JEAN:
HEY— YOU DON'T OWN HER
DON'T TRY TO CHANGE HER IN ANY WAY

SUZY:
YOU DON'T OWN HER
DON'T TIE HER DOWN, 'CUZ SHE'LL NEVER STAY

BETTY JEAN, CINDY LOU, and SUZY move back.

MISSY:
AND DON'T TELL ME WHAT TO SAY
AND DON'T TELL ME WHAT TO DO
JUST LET ME BE MYSELF
THAT'S ALL I ASK OF YOU
I'M YOUNG, AND I LOVE TO BE YOUNG
I'M FREE, AND I LOVE TO BE FREE,
TO LIVE MY LIFE THE WAY I WANT
TO SAY AND DO
WHATEVER I PLEASE
YOU DON'T OWN ME

BETTY JEAN:
YOU DON'T OWN HER

MISSY:
YOU DON'T OWN ME

SUZY:
YOU DON'T OWN HER

MISSY:
YOU DON'T OWN ME

CINDY LOU:
YOU DON'T OWN HER

MISSY:
YOU DON'T OWN ME

BETTY JEAN, CINDY LOU & SUZY:
YOU DON'T OWN HER

MISSY:
YOU DON'T OWN ME!

Applause.

BETTY JEAN moves down to Mr. Lee, palming the hidden Dream Catcher.

BETTY JEAN *(to Mr. Lee)*: Did you get all that? *(She then has a quick whisper with Mr. Lee)* What? You've got the Dream Catcher!

She crosses back up, bringing the old Dream Catcher with her and handing it to MISSY.

You must have left it over at his place.

The girls react to this.

CINDY LOU & SUZY: At his place.

MISSY: That's where we had pizza last.

BETTY JEAN, CINDY LOU & SUZY *(gently mocking her)*: Pizza.

MISSY: Bill, didn't you see me looking all over for this? Why didn't you just speak up and...

She lifts one flap; a ribbon drops dangling a ring.

SUZY: Look! Look!

CINDY LOU: It's a ring!

MISSY swoons and faints, legs slightly open.

BETTY JEAN gets the Dream Catcher and the ring.

SUZY: Oh Missy, close your legs. You're missing it.

SUZY fans MISSY and closes her legs. CINDY LOU grabs a glass of water and flicks some on MISSY's face. When MISSY comes to and SUZY helps her up, BETTY JEAN gives the ring to MISSY, who slips it slowly on her finger.

MISSY: Oh Bill!

SONG #18: WITH THIS RING

(Singing)
WITH THIS RING I PROMISE I'LL
ALWAYS LOVE YOU, ALWAYS LOVE YOU
WITH THIS RING I PROMISE I'LL
ALWAYS LOVE YOU, ALWAYS LOVE YOU

GOT NOTHIN' BUT THIS WHOLE HEART OF MINE
BABY PLEASE BELIEVE IN ME
OH, BILL, YOU KNOW SWEETHEART
I'LL ALWAYS TRY
TO KEEP YOU SATISFIED 'CUZ

MISSY (CONT'D):
WITH THIS RING I PROMISE I'LL
ALWAYS LOVE YOU, ALWAYS LOVE YOU
WITH THIS RING I PROMISE I'LL
ALWAYS LOVE YOU, ALWAYS LOVE YOU

> *BETTY JEAN crosses down and out to Mr. Lee.*

> *(Speaking)*

You thought you got out of coming up here again, didn't you? Not a chance...

> *BETTY JEAN brings Mr. Lee front and center and MISSY holds on to him.*

> *(Singing)*

WITH THIS RING I PROMISE I'LL
ALWAYS, ALWAYS LOVE YOU
WITH THIS RING
YOU GAVE ME A RING, YEAH

> *(To audience)*

HE GAVE ME A RING!

> *BETTY JEAN, CINDY LOU and SUZY get wedding bouquets.*

BABY, NEVER THOUGHT SO MUCH LOVE
COULD FIT IN A LITTLE BAND OF GOLD
BUT I'M TELLING YOU DARLING
I FEEL IT IN MY HEART
I'VE GOT IT IN MY SOUL

> *BETTY JEAN places MISSY's veil on her, and they all begin a wedding march downstage with Mr. Lee in tow as MISSY quickly and demandingly instructs Mr. Lee.*

> *(Speaking)*

March!

> *(Singing)*

WITH THIS RING YOU PROMISE YOU'LL
ALWAYS LOVE ME, ALWAYS LOVE ME

> *(Speaking)*

Right?

BETTY JEAN, CINDY LOU & MISSY:
WITH THAT RING YOU PROMISE YOU'LL
ALWAYS LOVE HER, ALWAYS LOVE HER

MISSY:
YOU KNOW THAT I LOVE YOU, BABY
WITH ALL OF MY HEART

ALL:
> WITH THIS RING I PROMISE I'LL
> ALWAYS LOVE YOU, ALWAYS LOVE YOU

MISSY:
> ALWAYS
> LOVE YOU!

BETTY JEAN, CINDY LOU & S:
> MARRY YOU BILL!

> *The girls toss white confetti and all take a final "wedding photo" pose.*

SUZY: Smile, Mr. Lee!

> *A Production Assistant comes down front (from the house) and takes a Polaroid Photo of the group.*

> *During the applause BETTY JEAN takes him back to his seat.*

BETTY JEAN: Now you better rest up for tonight, 'cuz you're gonna have a lot more pizza!

MISSY: You better believe it!

> *She panther-growls at Mr. Lee.*

Rowr.

CINDY LOU: Congratulations you two!

> *SUZY brings the Dream Catcher to MISSY.*

SUZY: Come on girls— Let's Catch a Dream!

MISSY: Oh my gosh— I can't imagine it getting any dreamier than this, but yes— Let's Catch A Dream.

> *They all move in together and surround the Dream Catcher just as before.*

ALL: Let's Catch a Dream!!

> *They all laugh and giggle. MISSY operates the Dream Catcher.*

L-O-V-E-That-Spells-Love.

> *CINDY LOU allows BETTY JEAN to open the flap. MISSY holds it out for SUZY to read.*

SUZY: It's Betty Jean's turn!

> *BETTY JEAN heads straight for the wine at the refreshment table.*

> *MISSY, SUZY, and CINDY LOU set up their microphones on the platform.*

MISSY: It's the birthday girl!

They speak in quick succession.

*SUZY: Oh I can't believe we forgot that— Happy Birthday—!

*CINDY LOU: Oh that's right! Happy Birthday, Betty Jean!

*MISSY: Many happy returns—!

BETTY JEAN *(with wine bottle in one hand, glass in another)*: Yeah, yeah, yeah, happy birthday to me.

MISSY: Three questions: Are you in love?

BETTY JEAN: We can just skip this part.

MISSY: Now play along!

CINDY LOU, MISSY & SUZY: Are you in love?

BETTY JEAN: Yes.

SUZY: Is he someone we know?

BETTY JEAN: Yes.

CINDY LOU: Is he here tonight?

BETTY JEAN: None of your beeswax. *(Crosses to her microphone)* You know, Johnny and I are going on three years now. But a person would know that if they actually came to the damn wedding.

> *BETTY JEAN gives a sharp look to CINDY LOU.*

CINDY LOU: Betty Jean, if you'd just let me tell you...

> *BETTY JEAN puts up her hand and doesn't let her finish.*

BETTY JEAN: ...and most of you know that we've both been working down at Harper's Hardware since high school. I'm up in corporate sales now, Johnny's still in raw lumber. And then two weeks ago, he just up and quit.

> *The girls react.*

And last week he... he up and moved out of the house.

> *The girls react.*

I don't know what happened. Johnny says he needs some time alone. Some time to think. Well I've had plenty of time to think myself.

SONG #19: I ONLY WANT TO BE WITH YOU

Hey, Johnny!

> *(Singing)*
> I DON'T KNOW WHAT IT IS THAT MAKES ME LOVE YOU SO
> I ONLY KNOW I NEVER WANNA LET YOU GO
> 'CUZ YOU STARTED SOMETHING, OH CAN'T YOU SEE
> THAT EVER SINCE WE MET YOU'VE HAD A HOLD ON ME
> IT HAPPENS TO BE TRUE
> I ONLY WANNA BE WITH YOU

BETTY JEAN (CONT'D):
    IT DOESN'T MATTER WHERE YOU GO OR WHAT YOU DO
    I WANNA SPEND EACH MOMENT OF THE DAY WITH YOU
    OH LOOK WHAT HAS HAPPENED WITH JUST ONE KISS
    I NEVER KNEW THAT I COULD BE IN LOVE LIKE THIS
    IT'S CRAZY BUT IT'S TRUE
    I ONLY WANNA BE WITH YOU

    YOU STOPPED AND SMILED AT ME
    ASKED ME IF I CARED TO DANCE
    I FELL INTO YOUR OPEN ARMS

CINDY LOU, MISSY & SUZY:
    SHE DIDN'T STAND A CHANCE!

BETTY JEAN: Now listen Johnny—

> *BETTY JEAN bumps wildly to the percussion, giving herself a crick in her neck.*

    (Singing)
    I JUST WANNA BE BESIDE YOU EV'RYWHERE
    AS LONG AS WE'RE TOGETHER, JOHNNY, I DON'T CARE
    'CUZ YOU STARTED SOMETHING, OH CAN'T YOU SEE?
    THAT EVER SINCE WE MET YOU HAD A HOLD ON ME

ALL:
    NO MATTER WHAT YOU DO
    I ONLY WANNA BE WITH YOU

BETTY JEAN:
    I SAID

ALL:
    NO MATTER, NO MATTER WHAT YOU DO
    I ONLY WANNA BE WITH YOU

> *Applause.*

CINDY LOU *(looking, pointing toward the back)*: Hey— isn't that Johnny now?

BETTY JEAN: Where?

> *BETTY JEAN looks out for him.*

SUZY: Who's that with him?

MISSY *(with a gasp)*: It's Judy Carter!

CINDY LOU & SUZY: Judy Carter?!

BETTY JEAN: The Mole-head.

BETTY JEAN moves to the center.

BETTY JEAN (CONT'D):
I HOLD MY HEAD HIGH
EACH TIME YOU WALK BY
GIVE YOU A GREAT BIG SMILE
ALTHOUGH I WANNA DIE
BUT WHEN YOU'RE NOT IN VIEW
MY WHOLE HEART BREAKS IN TWO
AND THAT'S WHEN THE TEARS START
AND I START CRYIN'

THAT'S WHEN THE TEARS START
AND I START CRYIN'
THAT'S WHEN THE TEARS START
INSIDE I'M DYIN'

WHEN FRIENDS ARE NEAR ME
I START PRETENDING
TELL THEM I'M DOING FINE
MY HEART IS MENDING
BUT WHEN THEY'RE NOT AROUND
MY WHOLE WORLD TUMBLES DOWN
AND THAT'S WHEN THE TEARS START
AND I START CRYIN'
THAT'S WHEN THE TEARS START
AND I START CRYIN'
THAT'S WHEN THE TEARS START
INSIDE I'M DYIN'

BETTY JEAN watches Johnny move across the back of the room with Judy.

(Speaking)

Johnny...!

BETTY JEAN crosses to stage right.

(Singing)
DON'T THINK ABOUT YOU
SO MUCH IN DAYLIGHT
'CUZ WORK IS ON MY MIND
AND I'LL MAKE IT ALRIGHT

BETTY JEAN (CONT'D):
BUT WHEN THE SHADOWS FALL
OLD MEM'RIES COME TO CALL
AND THAT'S WHEN THE TEARS START
AND I START CRYIN'
THAT'S WHEN THE TEARS START
AND I START CRYIN'
THAT'S WHEN THE TEARS START
INSIDE I'M DYIN'
THAT'S WHEN THE TEARS START
AND I JUST CRY
OVER YOU!

> *Applause.*

> *CINDY LOU crosses toward BETTY JEAN, trying to comfort her.*

CINDY LOU: Betty Jean, I'm so...

> *BETTY JEAN stops her in her tracks.*

BETTY JEAN: What?!

> *There is uncomfortable silence from all. CINDY LOU attempts to deflate the tension.*

CINDY LOU: Hey, come on— this is supposed to be a party, right? *(Tries to illustrate a party, arms in the air)* Whoo hoo... party...!

> *It's a slightly awkward moment.*

SONG #21: IT'S MY PARTY

> *First line should be spoken, then slow look to audience with reaction.*

BETTY JEAN *(ad lib, a cappella)*:
IT'S MY PARTY
AND I'LL CRY IF I WANT TO

> *Music in.*

CRY IF I WANT TO,
CRY IF I WANT TO
YOU WOULD CRY TOO IF IT HAPPENED TO YOU

MISSY & SUZY *(to Cindy Lou)*:
IT'S HER PARTY AND SHE'LL CRY IF SHE WANTS TO
CRY IF SHE WANTS TO, CRY IF SHE WANTS TO
YOU WOULD CRY TOO IF IT HAPPENED TO YOU

BETTY JEAN:

    NOBODY KNOWS WHERE MY JOHNNY HAS GONE

    BUT JUDY LEFT THE SAME TIME

    WHY WAS HE HOLDING HER HAND

    WHEN HE'S SUPPOSED TO BE MINE?

ALL:

    IT'S MY PARTY AND I'LL CRY IF I WANT TO

    CRY IF I WANT TO, CRY IF I WANT TO

    YOU WOULD CRY TOO IF IT HAPPENED TO YOU

BETTY JEAN:

    PLAY ALL MY RECORDS

    KEEP DANCING ALL NIGHT

    JUST LEAVE ME ALONE FOR AWHILE

    'TILL JOHNNY'S HOLDING ME TIGHT

    I'VE GOT NO REASON TO SMILE

ALL:

    IT'S MY PARTY AND I'LL CRY IF I WANT TO

    CRY IF I WANT TO, CRY IF I WANT TO

    YOU WOULD CRY TOO IF IT HAPPENED TO YOU

        *Music break, and BETTY JEAN goes out front toward Miss
        McPherson.*

BETTY JEAN: Miss McPherson— do you have a tissue, S'il vous plaît? Anything?
My mascara's starting to run!

        *MISSY, SUZY, and CINDY LOU react as they see Johnny and
        Judy come in at the rear of the house.*

MISSY:

    JUDY AND JOHNNY JUST WALKED THROUGH THE DOOR

        BETTY JEAN crosses back to her microphone.

BETTY JEAN: Where?

SUZY:

    LIKE A QUEEN WITH HER KING

CINDY LOU:

    OH WHAT A BIRTHDAY SURPRISE

CINDY LOU, MISSY & SUZY:

    HE'S NOT WEARING HIS RING!

        BETTY JEAN drags her microphone as she sings.

ALL:

    IT'S MY PARTY AND I'LL CRY IF I WANT TO

    CRY IF I WANT TO, CRY IF I WANT TO

    YOU WOULD CRY TOO IF IT HAPPENED TO YOU

BETTY JEAN:
   WHOA—
ALL:
   IT'S MY PARTY AND I'LL CRY IF I WANT TO
   CRY IF I WANT TO, CRY IF I WANT TO
   YOU WOULD CRY TOO IF IT HAPPENED TO YOU

   Applause.

   SUZY picks up the Dream Catcher.

CINDY LOU: Betty Jean, I really had no idea what was happening. I'm so sorry.

BETTY JEAN: I don't need your pity party, pink. What would you know about it, anyway "Miss Lucky Lips" boyfriend stealer...

   SUZY jumps between them, and BETTY JEAN angrily grabs the Dream Catcher from her.

   L-O-V-E-That-Spells-Love!!

   BETTY JEAN rips the Dream Catcher in two. She looks at one half, then the other, finally looking under the flap.

   (To Cindy Lou)

   It's your turn.

   BETTY JEAN takes the remains of the Dream Catcher away. MISSY tries to keep the mood happy and keep the party moving along.

MISSY: Three questions?

   MISSY waits for CINDY LOU to acknowledge, then continues.

   ...Are you in love?

CINDY LOU: Yes.

SUZY: Is he someone we know?

CINDY LOU: Oh yeah. You knew him.

BETTY JEAN: Is he somebody else's boyfriend?

MISSY: Betty Jean...!

CINDY LOU: No, it's alright. I've had it coming for ten years. Betty Jean— I've been wanting to tell you this for the longest time. Your wedding was beautiful, and you looked absolutely radiant.

   BETTY JEAN softens.

I was there, in the back. A person can change a lot in ten years, you know. *(Out to audience)* After high school I quit my job and left town as fast as I could. I wanted to be a movie star so I moved to Hollywood, California. Well, North Hollywood. After a few years I realized I didn't really want to be a movie star, I just wanted to be... somebody else.

CINDY LOU (CONT'D): When that finally hit me, I called Mr. Johnson at the Sweet Shoppe, got my old job back, and came back home. And right here in Springfield was the man who changed my life.

BETTY JEAN: Really? Who?

CINDY LOU: Remember the lead singer from the "Crooning Crab Cakes?"

SONG #22: SON OF A PREACHER MAN

Billy Ray Patton...?

The girls react to each other.

(Singing)
BILLY RAY WAS A PREACHER'S SON
AND WHEN HIS DADDY WOULD VISIT HE'D COME ALONG
WHEN THEY'D GATHER 'ROUND AND START A-TALKIN'
THAT'S WHEN BILLY WOULD TAKE ME WALKIN'
OUT THROUGH THE BACKYARD WE'D GO WALKIN'
THEN HE'D LOOK INTO MY EYES
LORD KNOWS TO MY SURPRISE
THE ONLY ONE WHO COULD EVER REACH ME

ALL:
WAS THE SON OF A PREACHER MAN

CINDY LOU:
THE ONLY BOY WHO COULD EVER TEACH ME

ALL:
WAS THE SON OF A PREACHER MAN

CINDY LOU:
YES HE WAS, HE WAS
OOH, YES HE WAS

BEING GOOD ISN'T ALWAYS EASY
NO MATTER HOW HARD I TRY
WHEN HE STARTED SWEET TALKIN' TO ME
HE'D COME AND TELL ME
EVERYTHING IS ALRIGHT
HE'D KISS AND TELL ME
EVERYTHING IS ALRIGHT
CAN I GET AWAY AGAIN TONIGHT

THE ONLY ONE WHO COULD EVER REACH ME

ALL:
WAS THE SON OF A PREACHER MAN

CINDY LOU:
THE ONLY BOY WHO COULD EVER TEACH ME

ALL:
WAS THE SON OF A PREACHER MAN

CINDY LOU:
YES HE WAS, HE WAS

MMM, LORD KNOWS HE WAS
HOW WELL I REMEMBER
THE LOOK THAT WAS IN HIS EYE
STEALIN' KISSES FROM ME ON THE SLY

CINDY LOU & SUZY:
TAKIN' TIME TO MAKE TIME
TELLIN' ME THAT HE'S ALL MINE

CINDY LOU & MISSY:
LEARNIN' FROM EACH OTHER'S KNOWIN'

CINDY LOU & BETTY JEAN:
LOOKIN' TO SEE HOW MUCH WE'RE GROWIN'

CINDY LOU:
THE ONLY BOY WHO COULD EVER MOVE ME

ALL:
WAS THE SON OF A PREACHER MAN

CINDY LOU:
THE ONLY BOY WHO COULD EVER GROOVE ME

ALL:
WAS THE SON OF A PREACHER MAN

CINDY LOU:
YES HE WAS, HE WAS
OOH, YES HE WAS

BETTY JEAN, MISSY & SUZY:
THE ONLY BOY WHO COULD EVER REACH HER
WAS THE SON OF A PREACHER MAN
THE ONLY BOY WHO COULD EVER TEACH HER

CINDY LOU:
HE WAS THE SWEET-TALKIN' SON OF A PREACHER MAN

CINDY LOU reveals a "Billy Ray" tattoo on her arm.

ALL:
YES HE WAS, HE WAS
OOH— YEAH
YES HE WAS

Applause segue.

SONG #23: *LEADER OF THE PACK*

The girls react to CINDY LOU's tattoo.

SUZY: Oh my golly! Is that a tattoo?

BETTY JEAN: Sure is.

CINDY LOU slips into Billy Ray's leather biker jacket. His name is emblazoned on the back, in a religious/crab motif.

MISSY: Is she still going out with Billy Ray?

BETTY JEAN: Well she's standing right over there. Let's ask her.

SUZY: Hey Cindy Lou, is that Billy Ray's jacket you're wearing?

CINDY LOU *(showing the back of the jacket)*: Uh-huh.

MISSY: Gee, it must be great riding with him.

BETTY JEAN: Is he picking you up after the reunion tonight?

CINDY LOU: Nuh uh.

BETTY JEAN, MISSY & SUZY: By the way, where'd you meet him?

CINDY LOU has crossed down right center with microphone.

CINDY LOU:
    I MET HIM AT THE CANDY STORE
    HE TURNED AROUND AND SMILED AT ME
    YOU GET THE PICTURE?
BETTY JEAN, MISSY & SUZY:
    YES, WE SEE
CINDY LOU:
    THAT'S WHEN I FELL FOR
ALL:
    THE LEADER OF THE PACK

CINDY LOU puts on sunglasses.

CINDY LOU:
    MY FOLKS WERE ALWAYS PUTTING HIM DOWN
BETTY JEAN, MISSY & SUZY:
    DOWN, DOWN
CINDY LOU:
    THEY SAID HE CAME FROM THE WRONG SIDE OF TOWN
BETTY JEAN, MISSY & SUZY:
    WHAT YOU MEAN WHEN YOU SAY
    THAT HE CAME FROM THE WRONG SIDE OF TOWN?
CINDY LOU:
    THEY TOLD ME HE WAS BAD
    BUT I KNEW HE WAS SAD

CINDY LOU (CONT'D):
THAT'S WHY I FELL FOR

ALL:
THE LEADER OF THE PACK

> *BETTY JEAN, MISSY, and SUZY put on sunglasses.*

CINDY LOU:
ONE DAY MY DAD SAID "FIND SOMEONE NEW"

BETTY JEAN, MISSY & SUZY:
NEW, NEW

CINDY LOU:
SO I HAD TO TELL MY BILLY WE'RE THROUGH

BETTY JEAN, MISSY & SUZY:
WHAT YOU MEAN WHEN YOU SAY
THAT YOU BETTER GO FIND SOMEBODY NEW?

CINDY LOU:
HE STOOD THERE AND ASKED ME WHY
BUT ALL I COULD DO WAS CRY
I'M SORRY I HURT YOU

ALL:
THE LEADER OF THE PACK

CINDY LOU *(dramatically speaking with the music)*:

He sort of smiled and kissed me goodbye.

The tears were beginning to show.

As he drove away on that rainy night,

I begged him to go slow.

Whether he heard me, I'll never know.

BETTY JEAN, MISSY & SUZY:
NO, NO, NO, NO, NO, NO, NO!

> *CINDY LOU crosses center.*

> *BETTY JEAN, MISSY, and SUZY cross up onto platform center.*

CINDY LOU: Lookout! Lookout! Lookout! Lookout!

> *There is a crash, with sound and lighting. BETTY JEAN, MISSY, and SUZY all face upstage.*

> *(Singing)*
I FELT SO HELPLESS WHAT COULD I DO?

BETTY JEAN, MISSY & SUZY:
DO, DO

CINDY LOU:
REMEMB'RING ALL THE THINGS WE'D BEEN THROUGH
AND STILL THEY ALL STOP AND STARE

CINDY LOU (CONT'D):
I CAN'T HIDE MY TEARS, BUT I DON'T CARE
I'LL NEVER FORGET HIM
ALL:
THE LEADER OF THE PACK
CINDY LOU:
THE LEADER OF THE PACK, AND NOW HE'S GONE
THE LEADER OF THE PACK, AND NOW HE'S GONE
THE LEADER OF THE PACK, AND NOW HE'S GONE
THE LEADER OF THE PACK, AND NOW HE'S GONE
BETTY JEAN, MISSY & SUZY:
GONE

Applause segue.

SONG #24: MAYBE

BETTY JEAN, MISSY, and SUZY sit on the edge of the platform. CINDY LOU crosses left of the platform.

CINDY LOU:
MAYBE, IF I PRAY EVERY NIGHT
YOU'LL COME BACK TO ME
AND MAYBE, IF I CRY EVERY DAY
YOU'LL COME BACK TO STAY
OH, MAYBE
BETTY JEAN, MISSY & SUZY:
MAYBE, MAYBE, MAYBE

CINDY LOU slowly takes off Billy Ray's jacket.

CINDY LOU:
MAYBE, IF I HELD YOUR HAND
I WOULD UNDERSTAND
AND MAYBE, IF I KISSED YOUR SWEET LIPS
I'D BE AT YOUR COMMAND
MAYBE
BETTY JEAN, MISSY & SUZY:
MAYBE, MAYBE, MAYBE

CINDY LOU holds the jacket tight to her chest.

CINDY LOU:
I PRAYED AND PRAYED TO THE LORD
TO SEND YOU BACK, MY LOVE
BUT INSTEAD YOU CAME TO ME

ALL:
ONLY IN MY DREAMS
CINDY LOU:
AND MAYBE, IF I PRAY EVERY NIGHT
YOU'D COME BACK TO ME
AND MAYBE, IF I CRY EVERY DAY
YOU'D COME BACK TO STAY
OH, MAYBE
BETTY JEAN, MISSY & SUZY:
MAYBE, MAYBE, MAYBE
CINDY LOU:
MAYBE
BETTY JEAN, MISSY & SUZY:
MAYBE, MAYBE, MAYBE

> *BETTY JEAN stands and moves closer to CINDY LOU.*

ALL:
MAYBE, MAYBE
MAYBE

> *Applause.*

> *BETTY JEAN opens her arms, and CINDY LOU embraces her. When they finish, MISSY rushes over and they all three share another big hug.*

> *When they break the hug, MISSY notices SUZY, who has crossed to the refreshment table.*

MISSY: Hey girls— it's Suzy's turn!

CINDY LOU: How could we forget Suzy?

BETTY JEAN: There's so much of her.

> *SUZY cries. MISSY comforts her, taking her to the microphone center.*

SUZY *(carrying her shoes)*: Does this make me look fat? I feel fat.

MISSY: Of course not, honey. You look just like the rest of us.

BETTY JEAN: Only bigger.

> *SUZY cries. CINDY LOU hits BETTY JEAN on the arm.*

MISSY: Maybe we should skip the three questions.

SUZY: Oh, okay. Well— I'm a housewife now. *(To the girls)* Yay.

BETTY JEAN, CINDY LOU & MISSY: Yay!

SUZY: And I'm going to have a baby. *(To the girls, less enthusiastic)* Yay.

BETTY JEAN, CINDY LOU & MISSY: Yay.

SUZY: Yay. We're going to have a little Ritchie Junior, right Ritchie, honey? *(Looks up for a response)* Ritchie?

> *They all hope to get a response, with none forthcoming. SUZY breaks into tears.*

SONG #25: SUZY'S MEDLEY:

[MAYBE I KNOW]

(Singing)
MAYBE I KNOW THAT HE'S BEEN CHEATIN'
MAYBE I KNOW THAT HE'S BEEN UNTRUE
BUT WHAT CAN I DO?

> *MISSY crosses over to BETTY JEAN and CINDY LOU and whispers with them.*

I HEAR THEM WHISPERIN' WHEN I WALK BY
"HE'S GONNA BREAK HER HEART AND MAKE HER CRY"
I KNOW IT'S ME THEY'RE TALKIN' ABOUT
I BET THEY ALL THINK I'LL NEVER FIND OUT

> *SUZY points up at Ritchie with one of her shoes.*

OH, MAYBE I KNOW THAT YOU'VE BEEN CHEATIN'
MAYBE I KNOW THAT YOU'VE BEEN UNTRUE

> *SUZY puts her shoes on.*

BUT WHAT CAN I DO?

> *SUZY crosses toward the others.*

(To Ritchie)
MY FRIENDS ARE TELLIN' ME THAT YOU'RE NO GOOD
YOU ARE NOT TREATING ME THE WAY YOU SHOULD
(Back toward girls)
"HE REALLY LOVES ME," THAT'S ALL I CAN SAY
BEFORE MY TEARS FALL, I JUST WALK AWAY

> *SUZY crosses back center.*

OH BABY I KNOW THAT YOU'VE BEEN CHEATIN'
BABY I KNOW THAT YOU'VE BEEN UNTRUE
BUT WHAT CAN I DO?
WHOA—

> *The following is almost unrecognizable through SUZY's tears.*

BABY I KNOW THAT YOU'VE BEEN CHEATIN'
BABY I KNOW THAT YOU'VE BEEN UNTRUE

SUZY (CONT'D):
BUT WHAT CAN I DO?

> *SUZY sits on the front edge of the platform.*

BUT WHAT CAN I DO?

> *Immediate segue.*

[NEEDLE IN A HAYSTACK]

> *MISSY crosses to SUZY, sitting next to her.*

MISSY:
WELL, WELL, I ONCE BELIEVED ALL FELLAS WERE NICE
GIRL, LISTEN TO ME AND TAKE MY ADVICE
YOU'D BETTER GET YOUR MAN
ON THE RIGHT TRACK
HE FOUND A GOOD THING AND THAT'S

BETTY JEAN, CINDY LOU & MISSY:
LIKE FINDING A

BETTY JEAN & CINDY LOU:
NEEDLE IN A HAYSTACK

> *MISSY stands.*

MISSY:
TELL HIM NOW, GIRL

BETTY JEAN & CINDY LOU:
NEEDLE IN A HAYSTACK

> *MISSY gets SUZY up, brings her back center.*

BETTY JEAN, CINDY LOU & MISSY:
YEAH, YEAH, YOU

> *BETTY JEAN and CINDY LOU dance over to join them center.*

SHA-DOO, WAH DAH SHOO
SHA-DOO, WAH DAH

CINDY LOU:
MOST FELLAS ARE

BETTY JEAN, CINDY LOU & MISSY:
SLY, SLICK AND SHY

CINDY LOU:
DON'T YOU EVER LET HIM
CATCH YOU LOOKING STARRY EYED

BETTY JEAN:
HE'LL TELL YOU THAT HIS LOVE IS TRUE
AND THEN WALK RIGHT OVER YOU

MISSY:
OH, YOU GOTTA TELL HIM NOW
BEFORE HE GETS OFF-TRACK
HE'S GOT A GOOD THING AND THAT'S
BETTY JEAN, CINDY LOU & MISSY:
LIKE FINDING A
BETTY JEAN & CINDY LOU:
NEEDLE IN A HAYSTACK
MISSY:
TELL HIM NOW, GIRL
BETTY JEAN & CINDY LOU:
NEEDLE IN A HAYSTACK
BETTY JEAN, CINDY LOU & MISSY:
YEAH, YEAH, YOU
SHA-DOO, WAH DAH SHOO
SHA-DOO, WAH DAH

MISSY crosses to her purse and pulls out SUZY's old prom queen crown and sash, now worn and slightly faded.

BETTY JEAN and CINDY LOU react with great joy as MISSY presents it.

MISSY:
HEY, HEY, HEY, HEY, HEY, HEY!

SUZY puts her sash on and turns back to the girls.

SUZY: It still fits!

She puts on her crown, and cries as she performs her "prom queen" wave.

MISSY:
OH—
YOU BETTER TELL HIM NOW
BEFORE HE GETS OFF-TRACK
HE'S GOT A GOOD THING AND THAT'S
BETTY JEAN, CINDY LOU & MISSY:
LIKE FINDING A
BETTY JEAN & CINDY LOU:
NEEDLE IN A HAYSTACK
MISSY:
TELL HIM NOW, GIRL
BETTY JEAN, CINDY LOU & MISSY:
NEEDLE IN A HAYSTACK

Immediate segue.

The girls return to their mics, leaving SUZY center.

[RESCUE ME]

SUZY *(following after Missy):* Oh, I don't know if I can...

> *MISSY turns her around and sends her back to her mic.*

MISSY: Oh no— get back there and tell him!

SUZY: Ritchie!

> *She sings simply, innocently.*

(Singing)
RESCUE ME
OH, TAKE ME IN YOUR ARMS
RESCUE ME
I WANT YOUR TENDER CHARMS
'CUZ I'M LONELY, AND I'M BLUE
I NEED YOU AND YOUR LOVE TOO
C'MON AND RESCUE ME

ALL:
C'MON BABY AND RESCUE ME

SUZY:
C'MON BABY AND RESCUE ME
'CUZ I NEED YA, NEED YA BY MY SIDE

ALL:
CAN'T YOU SEE THAT I'M LONELY?
RESCUE ME

SUZY:
C'MON AND TAKE MY HEART
TAKE YOUR LOVE
AND COMFORT EV'RY PART
'CUZ I'M LONELY AND I'M BLUE
I NEED YOU AND YOUR LOVE TOO
C'MON AND RESCUE ME

ALL:
C'MON BABY AND RESCUE ME

SUZY:
C'MON BABY AND RESCUE ME
'CUZ I NEED YA, NEED YA BY MY SIDE

ALL:
CAN'T YOU SEE THAT I'M LONELY?

> *Music vamps and segues.*

SUZY: I don't think he cares...

The girls rush over to SUZY center one by one.

MISSY: C'mon Suzy...

BETTY JEAN: You have his attention—

CINDY LOU: Now go in for the kill!

[RESPECT]

> *(Singing)*
> WHAT YOU WANT, BABY SHE'S GOT IT

BETTY JEAN:
> WHAT YOU NEED, YOU KNOW SHE'S GOT IT

MISSY:
> ALL SHE'S ASKING
> IS FOR A LITTLE RESPECT
> WHEN YOU GET HOME
> YEAH, BABY
> WHEN YOU GET HOME
> MISTAH!

SUZY:
> I AIN'T GONNA DO YOU WRONG
> WHILE YOU'RE GONE
> I AIN'T GONNA DO YOU WRONG
> 'CUZ I DON'T WANNA
> ALL I'M ASKING,
> IS FOR A LITTLE RESPECT
> WHEN YOU COME HOME
> BABY
> WHEN YOU COME HOME
> MISTER!
>
> I'M ABOUT TO GIVE YOU
> ALL OF MY MONEY
> AND ALL I'M ASKING
> IN RETURN HONEY
> IS TO GIVE ME RESPECT
> WHEN YOU GET HOME
> YEAH, BABY
> WHEN YOU GET HOME
> MISTER!

Music break. The girls all gather around SUZY to give her support. She removes her jacket. When she turns back around, she's gone from small and tentative to soulful and forceful.

SUZY (CONT'D):
OOH— YOUR KISSES
SWEETER THAN HONEY
AND GUESS WHAT?
SO IS MY MONEY
ALL I WANT YOU TO DO FOR ME IS
GIVE IT TO ME WHEN YOU COME
HOME
YEAH, BABY
WHEN YOU COME HOME
YEAH

SUZY now tries to spell it.

R-E-P-E-S-C-E...

She stops and thinks for a moment.

In quick succession:

MISSY: No.

CINDY LOU: Uh...

BETTY JEAN: That's not right...

SUZY figures it out.

SUZY:
R-E-S-P-E-C-T

BETTY JEAN, CINDY LOU & MISSY: That's it!

SUZY:
TAKE CARE, T-C-B
WHOA

BETTY JEAN, CINDY LOU & MISSY:
SOCK IT TO ME, SOCK IT TO ME
SOCK IT TO ME, SOCK IT TO ME

SUZY:
A LITTLE RESPECT, NOW

BETTY JEAN, CINDY LOU & MISSY:
SOCK IT TO ME, SOCK IT TO ME
SOCK IT TO ME, SOCK IT TO ME

SUZY:
WHOA

BETTY JEAN, CINDY LOU & MISSY:
  JUST A LITTLE BIT
SUZY:
  A LITTLE RESPECT, NOW
BETTY JEAN, CINDY LOU & MISSY:
  JUST A LITTLE BIT
SUZY:
  I GET TIRED
BETTY JEAN, CINDY LOU & MISSY:
  JUST A LITTLE BIT
SUZY:
  I KEEP ON TRYIN'
BETTY JEAN, CINDY LOU & MISSY:
  JUST A LITTLE BIT
SUZY:
  YOU'RE RUNNIN' OUT OF TIME
  AND I AIN'T LYING

  A LITTLE RESPECT
  YEAH
  WHEN YOU COME HOME NOW

  R-E-S-P-E-C-T
  FIND OUT WHAT IT MEANS TO ME
  R-E-S-P-E-C-T
  TAKE CARE, T-C-B!
    (Speaking)

You listen to me, Richard Lloyd Stevens: You know I love you, and I think I know you love me. But you've just gotta give me a sign... dammit!

> *The lights flash a pattern of red hearts all over the stage.*

> *Confetti canons may accompany this moment as well— as long as it is clearly noted that Ritchie is finally communicating his love for her.*

> *The girls jump up and down in celebration, and the lights pulse as the song moves into fever pitch.*

Wow!

    (Singing)
  RESCUE ME
  C'MON AND TAKE MY HEART
  TAKE YOUR LOVE
  AND COMFORT EV'RY PART

SUZY (CONT'D):
'CUZ I'M LONELY AND I'M BLUE
I NEED YOU AND YOUR LOVE TOO
C'MON AND RESCUE ME

C'MON BABY AND RESCUE ME
C'MON BABY AND RESCUE ME
'CUZ I NEED YA, NEED YA
BY MY SIDE
CAN'T YOU SEE
THAT I'M LONELY?
YEAH, RESCUE ME!

> *Applause. They gather together.*

ALL: We love you Ritchie!

> *The lights flash wildly.*

SUZY *(holding her belly)*: Oh! It kicked!

> *The girls gather around, feeling her belly. BETTY JEAN gets down close, yelling at SUZY's stomach.*

BETTY JEAN: Hello Ritchie Junior!!

> *SUZY pulls away from BETTY JEAN to protect her baby.*

MISSY: Oh wow— what a great reunion! Ritchie and Suzy are back together!

CINDY LOU: And I think I got my best friend back...

BETTY JEAN: Forever!

> *CINDY LOU and BETTY JEAN grab pinkies and hug.*

SUZY: And Missy is going to become Mrs. Lee! Or should I say Mrs. Chipmunk?!!

> *They make chipmunk faces toward Mr. Lee.*

> *They gather their mics and spread out across the stage.*

SONG #26: THANK YOU AND GOODNIGHT

CINDY LOU: Thank you all. This has been a terrific time!

> *They all put their jackets on.*

BETTY JEAN: Yes! Thank you so much.

SUZY: Thank you Ritchie.

> *The lights flash once.*

MISSY: Oh! Don't forget the cookie and punch reception over at the Elementary school!

ALL:

    THANK YOU AND GOODNIGHT
    THANK YOU AND GOODNIGHT
    THANK YOU AND GOODNIGHT
    THANK YOU AND GOODNIGHT

CINDY LOU:

    THANK YOU, FOR SHOWING US A WONDERFUL TIME
    GEE, EVERYTHING JUST TURNED OUT SO FINE
    SO THANK YOU AND GOODNIGHT

ALL:

    THANK YOU AND GOODNIGHT
    THANK YOU AND GOODNIGHT

BETTY JEAN:

    GEE, BUT IT'S FUNNY
    HOW THE HOURS SEEM TO GO BY SO FAST
    I ONLY HOPE THAT THIS TIME WON'T BE OUR LAST
    WE WANNA SEE YOU AGAIN

ALL:

    WE'D LIKE TO SEE YOU AGAIN

MISSY:

    I'VE NEVER FELT THIS WAY BEFORE
    AFTER A VERY FIRST DATE
    I NEVER KNEW WHAT JEWELRY COULD DO

ALL:

    GEE BUT THE FEELING IS GREAT

SUZY:

    OH BABY, IT'S GETTING LATE AND WE GOTTA GO
    HERE'S SOMETHING THAT YOU OUGHTA KNOW
    WE'VE HAD THE TIME OF OUR LIVES

            The mirror ball comes on.

ALL:

    THANK YOU AND GOODNIGHT

            Multi-colored tissue paper confetti flutters down from above.

    THANK YOU AND GOODNIGHT
    THANK YOU AND GOODNIGHT
    THANK YOU AND GOODNIGHT
    THANK YOU AND GOODNIGHT

            *They pick up their mics and return to their opening positions
            on the platform.*

    THANK YOU AND GOODNIGHT
    THANK YOU AND GOODNIGHT

ALL (CONT'D):
> THANK YOU AND GOODNIGHT
> THANK YOU AND...
>
> SINCERELY, OH YOU KNOW HOW I LOVE YOU
> I'LL DO ANYTHING FOR YOU
> PLEASE SAY YOU'LL BE MINE
> PLEASE SAY YOU'LL BE MINE

> *They take their final Wonderettes pose.*
>
> *Blackout.*

SONG #27: BOWS

PRINCIPAL (V.O.): Ladies and Gentlemen: The Marvelous Wonderettes!

> *Lights up for bows.*
>
> *The girls acknowledge Mr. Lee and Miss McPherson.*
>
> *MISSY gets the Polaroid photo taken earlier (now in a Wonderettes Photo Holder) and gives it to Mr. Lee.*
>
> *They acknowledge the band.*
>
> *Final Bows.*

SUZY: See you in 1978!

> *They all have a final wave as they exit.*

SONG #28: EXIT MUSIC

END OF ACT II

ABOUT STAGE RIGHTS

Based in Los Angeles and founded in 2000, Stage Rights is one of the foremost independent theatrical publishers in the United States, providing stage performance rights for a wide range of plays and musicals to theater companies, schools, and other producing organizations across the country and internationally. As a licensing agent, Stage Rights is committed to providing each producer the tools they need for financial and artistic success. Stage Rights is dedicated to the future of live theatre, offering special programs that champion new theatrical works.

To view all of our current plays and musicals, visit:

www.stagerights.com

Made in the USA
Columbia, SC
16 September 2020

20862627R00048